A Boy's Cottage Diary

1904

Annotated by Larry Turner

PETHERWIN
HERITAGE

Front cover: "Sunnybank" cottage in 1899-1900. Diarist Fred Dickinson is seated on verandah to the left of boy with tennis racket.

Back cover: "Sunnybank Pranks" shows Fred Dickinson behind his brother Tom, and below his cousin Harold during the summer of 1904.

A Boy's Cottage Diary, 1904

Published by Petherwin Heritage
60 MacLaren Street, Apt. 504
Ottawa, Ont., K2P 0K7
phone: (613) 231-5693
fax: (613) 231-5785
E-mail: lturner @ fox.nstn.ca
Home page: http://fox.nstn.ca:80/~lturner/

Copyright © 1996 Larry Turner

Artwork: Coral Nault
Book design: Wendelina O'Keefe
Cover design: Wendelina O'Keefe and Coral Nault
Editor: Patricia Stone
Map: Holly Dean
Production: Gail Pike, Creative Bound Inc.

Printed and bound in Canada by DFR Printing

Canadian Cataloguing in Publication Data

Turner, Larry
    A boy's cottage diary, 1904

Diary written by Fred Dickinson.
Includes bibliographical references
ISBN 0-9699381-1-X

    1. Dickinson, Fred--Diaries. 2. Beveridges Locks (Ont.)--Social life and customs. 3. Tay Canal (Ont.)--History. I. Dickinson, Fred II. Title.

FC3095.R535Z49 1996   971.3'82   C96-900305-6
F1059.R46T87 1996

Dedication

In Memory of Bessie and Tom Dickinson

Bessie and Tom at Sunnybank.

Other Books by Larry Turner

Rideau with John de Visser

Merrickville: Jewel on the Rideau

Ernestown: Rural Spaces, Urban Places

Rideau Canal Bibliography, 1972-1992

Perth: Tradition and Style in Eastern Ontario
with John J. Stewart

On a Sunday Afternoon: Classic Boats on the Rideau Canal edited with Alec Douglas

Historic Mills of Ontario
with Nick and Helma Mika

Voyage of a Different Kind:
The Associated Loyalists of Kingston and Adolphustown

Table of Contents

All illustrations, postcards and photos are in the author's collection except those marked PPC (Pethern Point Collection, a private archive) and those identified by a specific source.

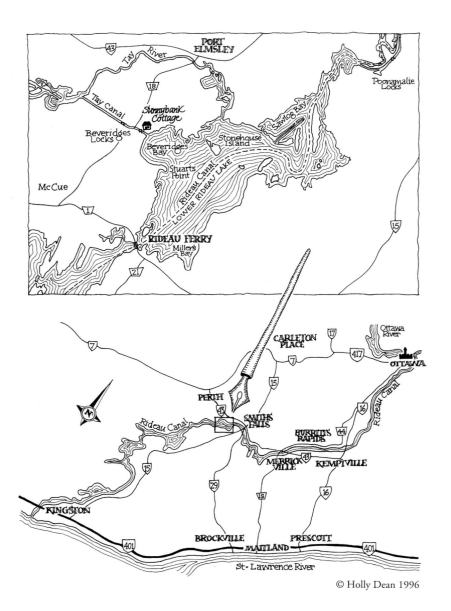

© Holly Dean 1996

Acknowledgements

The most important acknowledgement is to the young Fred Dickinson who wrote the diary and the family who preserved it. In an increasingly transient world, family memorabilia is frequently misplaced and forgotten, lost among the branches of a family tree. In constantly changing electronic cyberspace, the writing of diaries and journals is threatened by links in the chain of memory when storage in one system and one generation may be broken by the ability to retrieve it in another. The original diary is privately preserved as part of the Pethern Point Cottage collection, with copies deposited at the Rideau Canal Office, Smiths Falls, and the Archives of Ontario in Toronto.

Several individuals in the Perth and Rideau Lakes area contributed to the context of the diary. I enjoyed tapping the collected information and memories of Laura Armstrong, Mr. Brimmage, Peter and Susan Code, Murray and Kathryn Coutts, Gary Darby, Russell Griffith, Alan E. James, Mary McLean, Dick McVeety, the late Simon McVeety, Don Miller, Donald G. Oliver, and Ned and Wilma Winton. Others whom I consulted included Stuart M. Douglas, J. Sanderson Graham, Hugh Halliday, Janet Irwin, Eileen B. Jackson, Coral Nault, A. J. "Gus" Quattrocchi, Alan Rayburn, Alexander Reford, Maurice D. Smith, Elizabeth Stevens Stuart, and photographer Hugh Henderson at Pictures Perth.

I was aided in specific research questions by Christina Bates, Curator of Ontario History at the Canadian Museum of Civilization, John Bonser and Kathy Best at the Rideau Canal Office in Smiths Falls, Jill Shefrin at the Osborne Collection of Early Children's Books at the Toronto Public Library, and Jennifer Sullivan of the Children's Literature Service at the National Library of Canada. Curator Doug McNichol at the

Perth Museum provided access to the original un-microfilmed copies of the Perth **Expositor** newspaper for the year 1904.

I received gracious permission to quote from the poetry of Joan Finnigan **in the little brown cottage on loughborough lake** (Toronto, CBC, 1970) and from Paula Peterson's **Coming Home: An Intimate Glance at a Family Camp in the Adirondacks North Country** (Utica, North Country Books, 1993).

Within the family, my Grandfather, the late Tom Dickinson showed me "Sunnybank" before it was demolished, and Bessie Dickinson filled in some distant memories in her lifetime. I have dedicated this book to their memory. Fred's daughters, Marjorie Bleasdell, Dorothy Desautels, and Nancy McMillan were important sources of information, as was my mother, Frances Dickinson Turner.

I greatly appreciate the efforts of several people to bring this manuscript to publication. Patricia Stone of Peterborough, an accomplished author with two collections of short stories in print, edited my contributions with great care, and Julie Johnston of Peterborough and Rideau Lake, twice a recipient of a Governor-General's Award for children's literature, read the manuscript before publication. Holly Dean of Merrickville designed the map, Coral Nault of Brooke Valley contributed to the cover design and drew the figures, Wendelina O'Keefe designed the book, and Gail Pike of Creative Bound in Ottawa provided the production expertise.

Larry Turner
Petherwin Heritage
60 MacLaren Street, Apt. 504
Ottawa, Ontario
K2P 0K7

Preface

The annotation of this diary has been materializing over many years. At the family cottage at Pethern Point just a few miles west from Beveridges Bay, on the same chain of Rideau Lakes, the past is always present. The whole place evokes a living tradition in sense, smell and texture. Pictures, artifacts, furniture, tools, games, books, blankets, plates, and the dim light fixtures are constant reminders of a family tradition. It was a tradition of genteel ostentation, robust leisure and productive relaxation.

I can clearly remember visiting "Sunnybank" in my early teens with Tom Dickinson. I was not the listener I later became, but a connection was made between the building and the little diary written by his brother, Fred, stuffed in the drawer with the photographs. Some years later I went back to take a photograph. Evidently, the year after, the cottage was demolished, banished from the landscape and not a trace left behind. Yet so much remained in the musty diary and other photographs.

There is something unique about cottages in Ontario life. Where the nuclear families of the 20th century have scattered across the country following the lures of opportunity and the reality of employment, old family cottages have become those places, like gatherings at Christmas, where the family congregates once again. A huge proportion of Ontario cottages have been passed down through family, leaving a cluster of separate buildings on dwindling space, or an arranged time-share with surviving members. Cottages have become family anchors, shared experiences, keeping the ties that bind.

Where the urban environment is transitional, constantly changing, always in a state of becoming, cottage country offers an illusion. The lake, the trees and the cottage seem to stay the same (never the docks which are frequently displaced by ice).

But cottage country is also changing. Taking the generations of photos out of shoeboxes one sees the subtle transition of the changing landscape and skyline, not to mention the clothes and boats and paraphernalia of cottage life.

Cottages have kept families intensely conservative in their values of protecting water quality, shorelines, fish stocks, and wild spaces. The NIMBY feeling (Not In My Back Yard) is perhaps no more vigilant than in cottage country. Just witness a reaction to lost loon nesting wetlands, developing shorelines, and boating capacity on lakes. Where urban environments are subject to change, renewal, and displacement, the concept of the rural, the pastoral and cottage country have come to define a sense of place and meaning. It is this sense of a cultural landscape, rather than specific buildings, trees and lakes, that seems to resonate among cottage country activists. Yet so little has been written about the formative years of cottage life and recreational communities.

Fred Dickinson's diary is an early glimpse into the fun and activities that made cottage life such an enduring and significant factor in middle-class Ontario life. There is nothing in the diary that proclaims the experience as essential. One can surmise from later activities that it became so. The concept of the cottage in his time involved moving back to the land, back to nature, being with family separated by parents, work and school. The magic of the cottage experience was that it would happen again. In this little book, Fred Dickinson's summer of 1904 does just that.

Introduction

For a month in the summer of 1904, fifteen-turning-six-teen year-old Fred Dickinson had the time of his life at his grand-mother's cottage "Sunnybank" where the Tay Canal empties into Beveridges Bay on Lower Rideau Lake. It was a summer full of camping, fishing, boating, excursions and all around fun, the kind of summer experienced by youngsters in Ontario lakelands where families of country, town and city found relief from work-day life. Fred's experience is significant for what he captured in a diary.

For most kids, there would never have been enough time to enter the summer's activities in a diary, especially when it involved a carefree month at a family cottage sleeping under the stars or in a tent with brothers, cousins and friends. But Fred found time. His experiences are described in detail and involve the kinds of summer fun that refer back to an era of excursion

The lower lock at Beveridges Locks where the Tay Canal spills into its more famous cousin, the Rideau Canal. "Sunnybank" cottage was located 100 metres behind the tall pine tree. Photo by author, 1995.

steamers, new-fangled gasoline-powered boats, rustic camps, and rural landscapes.

Diary and journal entries are like short films with word symbols flickering mental and visual images. By interpreting the thoughts as they are expressed on paper and wrapping meaning around the message, readers enter the lives of the writer and capture fleeting moments of personal perception. The writer, in this case, Fred Dickinson, records impressions and feelings out of the ordinary or those that may be significant for him at that time or place. The challenge is to set in context the time and place when the entries were made and to understand how the world that is being described is similar or different to one's own perception of reality. The writer announces, "This is part of me at this time." The reader asks, "Who are you, what are you doing, and where is here?"

Summertime plays a large part in childhood memory because the sun is at its brightest, the days are at their longest, and for those who are lucky, life provides an adventure exploring forests and lakes. In Canada's northern climate, a few weeks of summer at camp or cottage are full of memorable experiences with friends and family in familiar surroundings. Every year those childhood reminiscences become sentimental journeys into star-lit nights, the path of a canoe, the tug on a fishing line, the call of whippoorwills and loons.

The book has three purposes: all ages will be fascinated by Fred's experiences set down in writing, as his diary represents a rare document written from the perspective of a youth. To encourage a sense of context in time and place, I have introduced each day's entry with an explanation of the activities. The diary itself is totally unabridged. It will be read by people seeking the thoughts of young people who lived in that era, and by others to gain a sense of summer recreation in the lakelands of Ontario when the experience of the cottage holiday was relatively unique. Most importantly, it will be read by young people themselves to get a mind's eye view of a different time.

The second purpose is to set the diary in context with the Edwardian era[1] and the Rideau Lakes system where it was written. A second section of three chapters explains lakeland recreation and cottages at the beginning of the 20th century, the role of local canals and communities, and the boats that Fred Dickinson would have seen while on the lakes. Period photographs from the family collection embellish the diary and provide another perspective on experiences.

A third purpose is to provide some texture and personality to the people and families touched by Fred's experiences. An effort has been made to trace the families mentioned in an epilogue and within detailed endnotes provided for the diary and the chapters. These references just touch the surface of a complex web of interaction which help define a community and a sense of place.

Breastworks at the upper lock at Beveridges Locks. The building of the Second Tay Canal between 1882 and 1891 linked Perth to Lower Rideau Lake. Photo by author, 1995.

The book will serve a market of young readers, cottage enthusiasts, and people interested in Ontario lakelands and the history of the Rideau corridor. It can provide local historians and genealogists with an example of how stories and lives of families can be shared with a wider audience. It will provide an authentic perspective on recreational history and the way people created and spent leisure time— an area of interest only recently explored. Fred's experiences link changing uses of Ontario waterways from commercial highways and economic gateways to recreational venues and cultural landscapes for tourists.

Fred Dickinson (right) with his half-brother Benjamin. Photo, PPC, c1908.

Fred's diary captures a moment in time, a thin slice of a year when having fun was the basis for being. It is an active diary, not reflective, and so it engages our imagination to fill in details and circumstance. Long buried in a shoebox full of photographs and later cottage journals, this diary emerges not as a dusty artifact, but as a fresh and challenging portrait of one boy's summer experience and what it was like to be young in the summer of 1904.

In this diary we are like listeners in the darkness outside the ring of a campfire, intent on a story being told by a young man to friends and family. It is a story of hope, excitement, adventure, longing, and the everyday patterns of a kid on vacation. In the words of Joan Finnigan **in the little brown cottage on loughborough lake** (Toronto, CBC, 1970):

Marshmallows on the twigs in the moonlight
and the children's folk-singing by the fire
floating across the lake
to the silence of the unseen listener
on the other shore

The Diary of Fred R. Dickinson

Frederick Roy Dickinson was born August 2, 1888 in Perth, Ontario, the eldest son of Benjamin Furney Dickinson and Ida Clarinda Hicks. When Fred arrived in Perth on Wednesday 27 July 1904, he was a few days away from his sixteenth birthday. Part of the Hicks family was living at "Sunnybank" cottage by the Beveridges Locks, and the other at the North Street house in Perth.

The Cast: (See epilogue and notes for more information)
• Thomas Sr. and Elizabeth James Hicks (Grandpa and Grandma) were parents to Lizzie, Tillie, Ede, Min, and Will (Tom Jr. was working in New York and Fred's mother Ida, was deceased). They alternated at the cottage, Tillie while on holidays from her job in Ottawa, Will on weekends and certain evenings after work at the family carriage-making business, and Lizzie, Ede, and Min handling the kids of "Beaver" camp as well as young Tom and Bessie Dickinson.
• Lizzie (Elizabeth Jane McCarthy), the original owner of "Sunnybank" cottage in 1899, who was widowed in 1900, was in charge of the household. She was accompanied by her son Harold (the same age as Fred) and daughter Etta (Ettie).
• Grandpa Hicks had been deposited at the cottage for the summer, and Grandma made the odd foray to the cottage from home. They had invited Fred, Ernest, Tom and Bessie Dickinson, their grandchildren, to visit for a month's vacation. Fred's cousins were at the cottage, along with Edmund Code, a close family friend, just two years younger than Fred and Harold.

(Reference to "walk ons" in the diary are discussed in

endnotes, square brackets are used to correct a word or name in the original text.)

The Setting:

"Sunnybank" cottage, was a rustic single-storey building owned by the family since 1899, adjacent to the lower lock at Beveridges Locks on the Tay Canal. The canal connected Perth to Beveridges Bay on Lower Rideau Lake, one of the chain of Rideau Lakes that formed the headwaters of the historic Rideau Canal in Eastern Ontario.

The diary takes up 99 blue-lined hand-written pages in a 122 page leather bound journal inscribed with the word "Memos" on the cover. The burgundy memo pad is almost 6 1/2 inches by 4 inches (16mm by 10.5 mm). The hand-writing is clear and confident, the spelling mistakes few, and the grammar remarkably well formed. The only curious element in the writing style is Fred's insistance of writing in the third person, which creates a certain emotional distance in the description of some of the activities. One might mistake this diary as a strict school assignment on penmanship and composition. It is in reality a fascinating insight into the everyday life of a boy at a cottage in the summer of 1904—an authentic glimpse into the mind of a youth at play.

On the inside cover, Fred provides the following details.

Fred R. Dickinson

This book contains a short account of the month's visit we had on Rideau Lake at Grandpa's Cottage from July 27 to Aug. 26, 1904.

When the word "we" is used it generally refers to the campers who slept in the tent "Harold" "Ernie" "Fred" and "Edmund."

Wednesday 27 July 1904

Fred, Ernie, Tom and Bessie Dickinson arrive at Perth from Kemptville on a Canadian Pacific Railway coach all dressed in their Sunday best to meet their late mother's side of the family, the Hicks. Their anticipation of visiting the cottage on Lower Rideau Lake was heightened by seeing lock stations at Merrickville and Smiths Falls from the railway bridges over the Rideau Canal and then passing Elmsley Station close to Port Elmsley on the Tay River. They knew the waterway linked Kemptville and Perth, as well as the cities of Kingston and Ottawa, but the railway cut a more efficient path between their parents and grandparents.

After being picked up at the squat stone railway station at the edge of Perth, they were taken to see their grandmother, Elizabeth James Hicks, who greeted them at the two-storey brick house on North Street. They were soon ushered to the family boathouse on the Tay River, just below the Basin between Drummond and Beckwith Streets. It was just a short ride down the Tay Canal to the Beveridges Locks and the location of the family cottage, "Sunnybank."

Will Hicks guides an unidentified family down the Tay Canal in the Bessie. Postcard, PPC, c1901-1903.

Because their aging Grandfather, Thomas Hicks Sr. suffered from rheumatoid arthritis, he could not meet them at the upper lock, but he was at the little cottage by the lower lock awaiting their arrival.

As all campers are aware, setting up the tent and comfortable sleeping quarters can be a challenge. Fred and Ernie Dickinson, their cousin Harold McCarthy and friend Edmund Code set up their tent near the cottage. The kids would have needed no introduction to mosquitos, but they probably had not anticipated the sheer quantity of these pests that were — and still are— attracted to weedy and shallow sections of Lower Rideau Lake. Unlike the upper lakes coddled deep in the ancient bedrock of the Canadian Shield, the lower lake introduced the low-lying, poorly drained Smiths Falls limestone plain. Wide pockets of drowned lands (formed by the flooding that allowed navigation on the Rideau Canal in 1832) made matters worse.

We arrived at Perth at half past one Auntie Ede and Harold meeting us at the station. After having a dinner at Grandma's we busied ourselves by taking a tent, blankets, eatables etc. to the boat-house. Edmund Code who lives in Perth owns the tent and it is a fine big one. At half past six Uncle Will, Mr Jack Griffith[2], Auntie Ede, Edmund Code, Harold and we [I] went to the cottage in Grandpa's Gasoline Yacht called the "Bessie." It is about seven miles to the lake and we got down in about 50 minutes. We did not lock through that night because Uncle Will and Mr. Griffith had to go back again. Auntie Min and Auntie Lizzie met us at the Upper Locks and we all walked down to the cottage carrying the baggage. Grandpa, unable to walk to the Locks was at the cottage and was very glad to see us. As it was getting quite dark we hustled around and put up and then made our bed of hay in it. On top of the hay we put oil-cloth and blankets and over us we had at least 10 blankets. Uncle Will and Mr Griffith returned then by moonlight. At half past nine Harold McCarthy (our cousin), Edmund Code, Ernie and Fred entered the tent sure of a good night's sleep. When we got nicely covered up about 50 squadrons of mosquitos molested the tent and anxiously hovered about our heads. To prevent being bitten by them we covered our heads with a blanket but the night was so warm that we could not stand the heat and had to disband our hiding-place and fight the unwelcomed intruders. We heard the other people going to bed at 10:15 and we lay awake till about 12 o'clock fighting the beasts when Edmund unable to resist their attacks clampered [sic] outside in his short tail and procured a lot of green grass and hay. After hunting for about 10 mins. for a match he lighted the fire to smoke the mosquitos out. He made the fire right at the foot of our bed and soon the smoke filled the tent. He quickly got outside but Harold, Ernie and Fred thought we could stand it. We put pillows on our heads but in about 5 min. we too were compelled to the open air. There the four of us sat in our bare feet and shirt tails in the warm summer's night and the moon shining brightly. The dense smoke hindered us from enter[ing] but in about 15 minutes we did so and were soon asleep. Before we went asleep we could hear some of the cottage folks out on the veranda as they were also attacked by the mosquitoes. They called to us a couple of times and asked us why we were not asleep but we did not answer.

Thursday 28 July 1904

The four boys, naming their site "Beaver Camp," had a friendly visit from Grandpa Hicks who provides some practical hints at making a more comfortable camp. Probably a veteran of fishing and hunting parties in much worse conditions, Grandpa was somewhat surprised with a tent with its own stove. The boys took part in three traditional activities of life by a lake: fishing, swimming and sailing.

The sailboat is likely a rowing skiff converted for sailing purposes when the wind rises. Lower Rideau Lake offers a wide expanse of water with few islands to get in the way. Fred and the others were fishing for largemouth and smallmouth bass, northern pike, pickerel (walleye) and smaller species such as yellow perch, rock bass, black crappies (shiners), and various other sunfish. The bathing place could be one of several sandy shallows, perhaps west on the north shore at the site of the present day Rideau Ferry Yacht Club beach and conservation area.

Thomas Hicks Sr. and Elizabeth James Hicks on the ivy-laden verandah of "Sunnybank." Photo, PPC, 1905.

At half past four after a sleep of about 4 hours we got up and dressed and then took the sailboat for a sail on the lake and also with the intention of catching some fish. When we got near the fishing grounds we saw that we had forgotten the anchor and so let the fish go. We then sailed to King's Point about a mile away. When we returned we had breakfast and it started to rain. We played games in the tent all morning and in the afternoon we took the sail-boat and the four of us sailed [to] the bathing-place for a swim. The bathing-place is an ideal place for swimming being all sandy bottom and a person can walk out 100 feet without going overhead. When we came back we made a stove out of stones and iron-sheeting which we found near the locks. Then Grandpa gave us some hints towards making a better bed and we rearranged our bed altogether. Edmund and I then built a clothes rack to hang our clothes on at night. After we got all this done it was supper time and we cooked our first meal at the "Beaver Camp."

Friday 29 July 1904

Fred provides a lot of detail today, a feature largely omitted in later entries in his diary. As you will see, for example, he provides the particulars of every day clean-up and descriptions of meals.

In 1904, the main meal, dinner, was eaten at lunch time; supper was the late meal of the day. Given that the family probably had a big meal for the children arriving at the cottage on Wednesday, the "force" that Fred refers to having been served at breakfast was a concoction dating back to medieval times but celebrated by Victorians as "fars," "farce," or "force-meat" which was ground meat, breading, savory and lard stuffing used in cooking a turkey, goose, duck or chicken. As leftovers, force could be rolled into balls or patties and fried for breakfast.

Pork and beans was a traditional Lanark favourite, whether in a lumber shanty in winter, or on a hunting trip in fall. Extra strong coffee also went with the campfire. One can just taste the juicy fresh raspberries plucked from the wild.

In 1899 Oliver's Ferry was renamed Rideau Ferry where the long swing bridge separated Big and Lower Rideau Lakes, and joined sections of the old Perth-Brockville Road, a pioneer artery. According to the Perth **Expositor** the boys witnessed an evening lawn social at the Coutts Hotel conducted by the Bethel Presbyterian Church at McCue, a hamlet located a short distance from Rideau Ferry. Tea was served from six to eight o'clock and refreshments were then offered (it was a temperance hotel) under the open sky in the presence of the Rideau band from Smiths Falls. Described as "one of the pleasantest and most profitable" socials of the season, it netted $76 for the church.[3]

After an excellent sleep we got up at seven o'clock and the fire-men Harold and Ernie put on a ripping fire in the stove for

"Sunnybank Pranks" was taken in front of the "Beaver" camp. Fred Dickinson appears to be cutting Tom's hair, while Harold McCarthy cavorts in a nightshirt carrying a lantern. Photo, PPC, 1904.

the cooks Edmund and Fred to get our breakfast. We had Force, boiled eggs, syrup, very strong coffee (I think we put in 2 1/2 tablespoonfuls of coffee), bread etc. After breakfast we washed and dried the dishes and put them away in our cup-board and then made the bed up. After this we went to the bush and gathered a lot of pine knots for fire wood. We stayed there till dinner time climbing trees and cutting branches with our jack-knives etc. We cooked a rattling good dinner and instead of having tea we made coffee by putting water into the remains from breakfast. After dinner we had a swim in the canal and then we picked two quarts of raspberries for supper. We then played quoites and nobbies. After this we had supper consisting of a tin of pork and beans, fried potatoes, cookies, biscuits, bread etc. and after supper the four of us went in the rowboat to Oliver's Ferry about 2 1/2 miles away. There happened to be a social there that night and the Smiths Falls band was there. After treating ourselves and procuring our provisions we started for home after nine o'clock. It was a bright moonlight night and we rowed home in 37 minutes. We had some grub before returning and were soon asleep.

Pine-knots refers to kindling and sticks of wood in the form of dead branches on older white and red pine trees as well as dry cones found at the base of trees.

"Quoits" is an ancient English game with its antecedent in the throwing of the discus and its transition into the game of horseshoes. The game involved throwing a perforated plate of iron, or hollow iron disc on to, or near, an iron pin called a "hob" driven into the ground from 16 to 20 yards away. From **The Boys Book of Sports and Games**, a Victorian publication: "Formerly, in the country, the rustics not having the round perforated quoits to play with used horseshoes, and in many places the quoit itself, to this day, is called "a shoe.""[4]

(The author's condescending remark about "rustics" in the English countryside would have been seen as a compliment by the Hicks family at their cottage.)

The game of "nobbies" is similar except that hoops made of rope were tossed at a distance on to wooden pegs. Points would not be given as to how close the hoops came to the peg, but the necessity of actually ringing the peg.

Saturday 30 July 1904

At a cottage you can get away from the humdrum chores of the city, but not the country. In the following account in his diary Fred complains about cooking and washing chores. The boys are busy most of the day pruning trees in the "grove," a shaded area by the cottage that can be seen in the accompanying photograph. They did have time to swim in the canal, catch a fish dinner, and go for a swift sail before an impending storm.

We awakened at half past seven and it was nice and cool so before dressing we put on our swimming pants and jumped into the canal for a swim. The water was fine and wakened us up. We then cooked breakfast and the cooks (who have all the work to do) had to wash and dry the dishes again. Edmund, Tom and Fred then went fishing and caught some for dinner. Grandpa then invited us all to trim up the trees in the grove. We worked at this until dinner time and did not think of getting dinner so the cottage people cooked our potatoes and fish for us on their stove. After dinner was over and the dishes washed we took our blankets in off the fence where they had

The Hicks, Dickinson and McCarthy families with friends relax in the nearby grove. Fred Dickinson is lying on the ground with his head supported by his hands in the middle of the photograph; Harold McCarthy is just behind him, who is just in front of his Grandpa and Grandma Hicks. Note the hammocks and rustic lawn furniture. Photo, PPC, Sept. 1899.

been airing and made up our bed as it looked like rain and then we went for a sail. There was a very strong wind and our boat went spinning along. We never had such a fast ride in one. We then trimmed the trees up till supper time and after supper we played foot-ball and went for another sail.

Sunday 31 July 1904

By the beginning of the 20th century, rules governing the Sabbath Day slowly loosened, allowing for a wider interpretation of a day of rest. This was a new era of cottage life, the rise of the weekend, and a new awareness that a day of rest also meant recreation.

The "Bessie" boat makes its appearance, the first reference to the earliest motorboat using an internal combustion engine on the Rideau Lakes in 1901. (More information on the Hicks' vessel is provided in section 2, chapter 3, on boating.)

Everyone who has camped in the Ontario lakelands knows

the sound and fury of a summer storm with its dazzling lightning, booming thunder, drenching rain and gusts of wind.

We did not waken till about 9 o'clock and when we were half dressed Mr. Bob Meighen rowed here from the Ferry to meet Mr. Charles Meighen[5] and Mr. Bob Smith[6] who were coming down in the "Bessie" boat this morning with Uncle Will. After he waited at the cottage for half an hour the yacht arrived and the three of them rowed to the Ferry. We did not get our own breakfast cooked till after ten. Uncle Will, Bessie, Edmund and Fred then went for choke-cherries while Harold, Ernie and Tom went for a sail. When we came back it was one o'clock and we fixed up a lunch of sandwiches and buns and went for a stroll across the locks and half way up King's Point.[7] We took Tom with us and the five of us had a good dinner under a large maple tree. After our lunch we walked around exploring the land, cutting our names on trees and getting up in trees to get the cool fresh breeze from the lake. At half past two the beautiful rain fell in torrents and we sought shelter under the trees. It rained so steady that the trees would not keep it off us so we had a fine bath. It rained nearly an hour and after it stopped we started home. Luckily we did not have our Sunday clothes on. We changed our clothes and we were all right again. We read till it was time to have supper and along with the help of the cottage folks we had an exhorbitant meal consisting of "canned tomatoes," "canned pork and beans," "corned beef and tongue," "potatoes," beets, mustard, tea, soda biscuits, cookies etc. When we got the table set it started to rain so we put it in the tent. The wind blew and shook the tent like fun, the thunder roared but all the same we had a slick supper.

Choke cherries were the fruit of a common variety of brush in the area that grew in open clearings, along streams and the borders of wooded areas. They were so popular that some of Perth's amateur sports teams were so named, such as the Perth Choke Cherries lacrosse team until 1893.

Monday 1 August 1904

Wherever there are locks on the Rideau Canal there are "lock-rats"—local children fascinated with the rushing water through waste weirs, flushing sluices, groaning lock gates, noisy cast-iron crabs, and hand-operated mechanisms such as rack and pinion gears. And there was an endless fascination with the boats themselves—vessels of all shapes and sizes—and the often friendly banter between lock staff and boat operators.

"Sunnybank" cottage in its first or second year. Note the board and batten siding, cedar-shingled roof, and awnings providing shade for the verandah. Left to right, Ettie McCarthy, Edith (Ede) Hicks, Bessie and Ernest Dickinson, Annie (Tillie) and Minnie Hicks, Harold McCarthy, Fred and Tom Dickinson (with tennis racket), Elizabeth (Lizzie) McCarthy. Photo, PPC, c1901.

"Lock-rats" were particularly excited by commercial barges and steamers. A commercial boat meant a free ride through the locks, helping deckhands with the lines, and even the lockmaster and lockmen at their duties.

At Beveridges Locks, the ride included an upper and lower lock separated by a few hundred yards of canal excavation. Fred took a ride on a sailing barge and played in the wake of the opulent Edwardian steamers, the **Rideau King** and **Rideau Queen**, of which more will be said in chapter three on boating.

The children also saw the steam tug **Shanly** commanded by the genial Frank Nevins. The tug was part of the Rideau Canal floating plant including dredges and scows that were used to maintain the waterway.

We got up at 8 o'clock and at once got breakfast. We then commenced firing the bed-clothes out and washing the dishes. Grandpa then gave us another invitation to trim up the trees and we worked at it till dinner time. After dinner the "Mary Louise" a large sailing barge locked through going to Perth with a load of cheese-boxes. We jumped on and went up to the upper locks on it. When we came back we worked at the trees till 3 o'clock and then had a fine swim in the canal. I swam to the locks and back (about 400 feet). After the swim we sailed to the Ferry for provisions and Grandpa gave us some "cash" to buy ice cream with. After spending some time at the Ferry the government yacht the "Stanley" [Shanly] came in with a barge of lumber. On our way home the "Rideau King" and "Queen" passed us going to Ottawa. We rowed up close to them and got their swells [wake] also had a good look at them. We arrived home at 8:15 and had some supper. Little Tom caught two large mud-pouts [catfish] each over a foot long, a 4 pound black [smallmouth] bass, a large pike, a shiner and numerous sunfish and rock bass tonight.

Tuesday 2 August 1904

One is reminded that cottage life in 1904 is an extension of the town into the countryside. The boys are doing camp chores, and their female relatives are doing their washing. The lakeland offered a change in venue, but it often made domestic activities, especially for women, more difficult. Instead of running water from the town system, the ladies of the cottage had to rely on hand-delivered resources in a setting much less convenient than home. Look at what the women are wearing at the cottage site in the photographs (even if they are perhaps more dressed up for the camera)! The long dresses, undergarments and frills all had

Grandma Elizabeth James Hicks strolling the cottage grounds. Photo, PPC, 1904.

to be hand-washed, dried, and then worn in a landscape full of clinging seeds, and in boats full of fish brine and bilgewater. Long dresses looked appropriate for the time on steamer excursions, but the reality of camp life eventually brought forward a change in outdoor wear.

(No mention is made of birthday celebrations for Fred, if any, who just turned 16.)

(my birthday)
We got up at 7 o'clock and after breakfast Edmund, Tom and Fred cleaned Tom's fish while Ernie and Harold washed the dishes and carried water for the ladies to do the washing with. We then finished our job in the grove and went fishing and sailing. Grandma and Mrs. Jim McCallum[8] drove Nellie out from Perth this morning. After dinner the "Mary Louise" locked through. Ernie and Harold then took Mrs. McCallum and Auntie Min for a sail in the sail-boat. They went about 4 miles. When they returned Mr. Bob Meighen who came from the Ferry to see Grandpa for the afternoon took the campers for a sail in his sail-boat. He is a good sailor and gave us some hints on sailing and when we returned we sailed in our own sailing boat to the bathing place for a swim. We had supper when we returned and played games until bed time.

Wednesday 3 August 1904

Another day on the Rideau fishing and swimming. Contemporary photographs reveal the grove withs its attendant hammocks and swings. It was a lazy, shady place protected from the sun but strategically placed to allow south-westerly breezes to keep the flies down.

After breakfast we were fishing and caught some black bass. We then played quoits until dinner time and after dinner raked the grove and fixed the swings and hammocks. At two o'clock all the boys went to the bathing place. We had a fine swim. We took the big boat out a long piece from the shore and turned summer-saults [sic], jumped and dove off it. When we came back we read until supper time and after supper we picked a quart of berries. We put a smudge in the tent and did not have a mosquito.

One of Ettie's friends at "the bathing place" on Lower Rideau Lake. Photo, PPC, c1904.

Thursday 4 August 1904

A common pursuit of vacationing is sleeping in, and the boys are caught doing so today. However, in the Edwardian era frought with purpose and practicality, Fred tempered his account with the verb "hustled" in the desription of getting breakfast.

We were rather late getting up but we soon hustled up the breakfast. I made some rolled oats porrage [sic], boiled some eggs etc. and after breakfast we worked at odd jobs for a short

*time and then all the boys went to Mr. McVittie's Farm⁹ to dig
a pail of worms for fishing purposes. When we were getting the
worms Auntie Lizzie, Ede, Min, and Bessie and Tom rowed to
the bathing-place for a bath. We all got back at dinner-time
and after dinner the boys sailed to the bathing place and had a
'ne time for about an hour. When we returned we had an
early supper and the camp boys rowed to the Ferry for provisions. We had two large bottles of birch beer, peanuts and candy
and about 9 o'clock returned in the dark.*

We have no indication of the effects of birch beer, a concoction
of birchsap and honey described as having "a kick like a mule" and
"definitely not suitable for children."¹⁰

**The Rideau Ferry bridge with a swing section in one of its six spans formed
an effective barrier between Lower and Big Rideau Lakes. The Coutts House
Hotel is visible on the skyline of this recreational community. Postcard,
c1900-1907.**

Friday 5 August 1904

Sailing can be a test of skills in the best of weather, and the
boys narrowly escaped a grounding on a shoal. They were heading to Miller's Bay in the south-west corner of the lake where
Robert Miller sold produce locally.

Lockmaster Daniel Buchanan was a permanent resident, neighbour and friend who resided at the lockmaster's house at Beveridges Locks. The two-storey prefabricated lockmaster's house was erected in 1884, an early example of a module home assembled on the site. At that time the lockmaster kept a garden, a few cattle and horses, and blended in with the everyday life of the area. He was lockmaster at Beveridges Locks from 1902 to 1924.

Between the Drummond and Beckwith Street Bridges, the Hicks family built a boathouse in the 1890s to take advantage of the Tay Canal's access to the Rideau Lakes. Postcard, c1900-1905.

We got up early and after breakfast Ernie went and got Mr. Buchanan, the Lockmaster's horse and drove Auntie Lizzie and Grandpa to Perth. He stayed in Perth and had dinner returning home himself after tiding up the back-yard and fixing things up Harold, Edmund and Fred sailed to Mr. Miller's for butter.[11] There was a very high wind blowing and the waves were quite high. When we got on the lake and put up the sail and went like chain-lightning. Fred was pilot and we were going so fast that Fred could hardly turn the rudder. Soon we were within 100 yards of the shore and Harold tried to let down the sail. As he was doing so the wind caught on the top of the mast. It

*wheeled around and the poles caught in the front of the boat.
We did not know what to do. Fred tried to steer at right angles
with the wind but was unable to. We were going very fast and
soon would be on the rocks. Edmund and Harold both worked
at the sails and when we were only a few yards from shore
Edmund pulled the mast down and sail and all fell just in time
to save the boat from a good deal of damage. It was quite exciting for a few minutes but after all we floated in nicely. In the
afternoon we tidied up things and played games till bedtime.*

Saturday 6 August 1904

For those who still have to tangle with the periodic cleaning
of stove pipes leading from a wood stove to a chimney, one can
sympathize with the boys. After dismantling the cottage cluster
with clouds of black soot everywhere, and different lengths of
stove-pipe strewn indoors and out, everything had to be returned
to its place as in an elaborate puzzle. And nothing seemed to go
back the way it was. There were two stoves to handle.

The Beveridges Locks were never a busy station as the commercial use of the Second Tay Canal was limited. Although some
boats kept schedules, most arrived out of nowhere and sounded
their steam whistles, if they had them, to warn the lockmaster of
their impending arrival. Whistles were important on the Tay
because the lock staff could be some distance at the upper or
lower lock when a boat approached out of view. On this day
Lockmaster Daniel Buchanan was caught short-staffed just when
he had boats at opposite ends of the locks.

Fred and Edmund took delight in their role as deputized
lockmen. The lockmaster opened the gate sluices in the lower
gates to release water in the lock chamber while it reached the
level of the lake. Fred and Ernie then swung the lower gates by
means of a crab using an endless chain mechanism manipulating
either a long swing bar or push bar attached to the gate. The
gates were either built of oak, the favoured lumber until
resources ran out, or, if renewed since 1896, Douglas Fir from

British Columbia. The gates were swung on a vertical heel post rotating on a gate pivot and anchored by a massive iron collar and heel band set in the lock walls.

After the steam barge **Westport** was let into the chamber, the boys closed the gates, the lockmaster closed the gate sluices and then released water through sluices in the stone walls located by the upper gates to refill the chamber. Fred and Ernie then opened the upper gates when the lock was full allowing the barge into the channel leading to the upper lock. Lockmaster and helpers then rushed to the upper lock where the barge would rise again to a level that would take the craft to Perth.

Harold's sister Etta Catherine (Ettie) McCarthy was accompanied in the **Bessie** by Richard McCarthy, an Uncle of their late father.[12]

We slept till eight and after having breakfast we all got to work and took down the stove-pipes in the cottage to clean them and replace some good ones. Sorry to say it took us till dinner time to fix them up again. We could not have got a tinsmith and it was "either get the pipes up" or "go without dinner." We raked around the tent and cottage nearby all day and in the evening we went to the locks to se the "Bessie" boat lock through. All except Auntie Ede, Tom, Edmund and Fred went to the Upper Locks to meet them. While Mr. Buchanan[13] *(the lockmaster) was at the Upper Locks waiting for the yacht*

Etta "Ettie" Catherine McCarthy was Harold's sister, and a few years older at age twenty, than the boys at the "Beaver" camp. Photo, PPC, c1904-07.

with Mr. McCarthy from Prescott and Ettie in it the Westport, a large steam barge blew for the locks. Mr. Buchanan had to hustle down and let all the water out as his assistant had gone to Perth just a while before. Edmund and Fred had to help him. We opened and shut the big gates. When we got to the Upper Locks Uncle Will was there waiting to be locked through. After the yacht locked through we carried the valises etc. to the house and Mr. McCarthy gave the campers a big bag of cream candies. We had a feed in the tent before going to bed.

Sunday 7 August 1904

Everyone piled into the gasoline yacht for a cruise to Poonamalie Lock. The lock and dam form the outlet for the Rideau Lakes and the head of the Rideau River as it descends through Smiths Falls and winds it way to Ottawa. Poonamalie never developed the mills and bridges forming a central place for a community like other lockstations. Instead the channel leading to the locks is graced by a grove of white cedar trees.

Poonamalie Locks marked the outlet of the Rideau Lakes into the Rideau River. Poonamalie has retained a quiet rural charm, still distinguished by its cedar groves. Postcard, c1905-1907.

In his August 1905 article on "Fishing on the Tay" in **Rod and Gun in Canada**, F. W. Lee described his favourite picnic site at the lock: "a deep silence brooded over the place, save when the wind rustled through the green trees or the roar of the rapids on the other side was borne softened by the distance into a musical murmur."

In **Dr. Lake's Chart of the Rideau Lakes Route**, first printed by Dr. Elmer J. Lake in 1907, he described the run through Poonamalie as being "very beautiful with its trees along the water's edge, and its cedar-bordered walk on the north side above the lock." Lake also described the cut below the lock "lined with large cedars on each side overhanging the water, to whose depth of shade and beauty the camera with instantaneous shutter will do no justice."

The boys were not a part of a later cruise that day when Will Hicks took the launch through the swing bridge at Rideau Ferry and into Big Rideau Lake as far as the Rocky Narrows. There, Will's party visited Hogg's Bay, the site of the early sawmill built by Reuben Sherwood of Brockville between 1810 and 1820, presently within the boundary of Murphy's Point Provincial Park.

When entering Adam's Lake they may have noticed nearby a

The Hicks and Dickinson families are crammed on board the Bessie for a family outing at the foot of Beveridges Locks. Photo, PPC, 1904.

verdant peninsula where they would build their second cottage fifteen years later.

> *We all got up about 8 o'clock and after breakfast Mr. McCarthy, Ettie, Auntie Min, Uncle Will, Bessie, Tom and the campers took the yacht for a ride to the Poonamolee [Poonamalie] Locks about 6 miles down the lake. We got off there and viewed the beautiful scenery. We walked around in the groves and bushes as it is an exceedingly pretty place. We returned at noon and had dinner and after dinner all but the camp boys went in the yacht about 10 miles up the lake. They went into Hogg's Bay and Adam's Lake where the scenery is very fine. While they were away we took the sail-boat and went for a sail over the lake and also read books. We had our supper over before they got back and they did not have theirs till after seven.*

Monday 8 August 1904

This day is unique to canal life. Toy-boat making was a familiar pastime for boys living near placid stretches of water. The boys sailed model boats by setting them free, or keeping them on a line from the tow path between the lower and upper locks. This canal cut was oblivious to variable winds, and perfect for playing with model craft.[14]

Every lock had a makeshift raft used by lock staff for various purposes in summer. It became a diver's delight when pulled into the channel which allowed about five and a half feet of depth. Only good relations between a lockmaster and a neighbour would permit children to use canal property in this fashion.

The excitement of trip through the locks on a sailing barge was a "lock-rat's" heaven. Then to be invited to sail the whole length of the Tay Canal was icing on the cake. The boat captain would have seemed overly generous and kind to the four boys, but he was just as pleased to acquire four deckhands to help navigate the weedy reaches of the canal and to help with the lines in the basin.

It rained last night and the morning was fine and cool. Uncle Will went to Perth with the yacht before we were up and after breakfast we all busied ourselves making sail-boats. Harold and Ernie's were top heavy and they soon remedied the boats. Edmund's, Tom's and Fred's sailed up and down the cut fine. After dinner Auntie Lizzie, Ede, Bessie and Tom went fishing but had not very good luck while Ettie, Mr. McCarthy and Auntie Min rowed to "Rideau Ferry" and stayed till about seven. After we stopped sailing the boats we took the lock raft out into the middle of the canal and anchored it. We had a fine time diving off it and turning summer-sets [sic] into the water. After supper we made a camp fire near the tent and sat around it playing the mouth-organ and singing. Mr. McCarthy, Ettie and Auntie Min went for a walk and came back at 8:30. They also came and joined in the celebration. While we were having this revelry the large steam yacht Jopl towing a large barge Rover loaded with cheese boxes blew for the locks and immediately the boys put out the fire and made a bee-line for the locks. When the yacht came to the top of the lock we got on and as the barge was

Looking toward the Craig Street swing bridge, the Tay Canal tow path only continued until the ruins of Dowsen's Lock, a remnant of the First Tay Canal. Postcard, c1905.

put beside the yacht while locking through we could sit on the engine room windows and see the engineer running the engine. Both the pilot and engineer were very nice men and talked with us all the way to the Upper Locks. When we reached there the engineer asked us if we would be like to go to Perth in the morning as they were going to stay at the locks all night and leave at 5 a.m. We thanked him and told him we would probably go. They were going to return at noon and it would be a fine ride for us so we hustled home and asked the cottage folks for permission to go to Perth in the morning. They laughed at our intention of getting ready at 5 o'clock and were sure that we would miss our ride but nevertheless they said that we could go and we made up our minds to be ready in time. We got the alarm clock out of the cottage and after setting it for half past three we at once got to bed. It did not take us long to get asleep and we were making our plans for the next day in our dreams.

Tuesday 9 August 1904

Just as expected the master of the **Jopl** found his temporary deckhands a useful crew in helping with a disabled rudder. Perhaps the ulterior motive for the trip was the surprise visit to Grandma Hicks, who showered them with treats for their camp, and next door at the carriage shop where Will Hicks contributed some mad money for their town visit. An interesting sight for the boys was the steam yacht then under construction in Perth.

After a sound sleep the alarm rang at correct time and wakened us thoroughly as it rang about 5 minutes but it was so dark we could hardly see to dress so we lay awake till four o'clock. We then got up and the firemen put on a fine fire. The morning was cold and damp and there had been a very heavy dew. We appreciated the heat very much as we crowded round the stove while breakfast was cooking. I made a lot of porrage [sic] and it went fine on the cold morning and also boiled eggs and made coffee. We moved our table within two or three feet of the stove and greatly enjoyed the meal. We were in such a hurry that Fred burned all the end of his tongue trying to drink his coffee. At 10 minutes to five we had finished our breakfast and fired the pots and dishes any old place and then hustled to the Upper Locks. They had steam up and at 5.15 a.m. we started. It was so chilly and the sun had not risen that we sat in the engine room nearly all the way up and procured quite a lot of information from the engineer concerning the engine. We got into Perth at a quarter to seven and tied up in the basin. Harold Ernie and Fred went to Grandma's and she was very surprised to see us. She made us eat a second breakfast. After

The revitalization of the Tay Basin with the opening of the Second Tay Canal ushered in a wave of civic pride. The Perth town hall can be seen beyond the Drummond Street Bridge. Postcard, 1905.

breakfast we watched the steam drills at work and the men blasting at the sewerage. We then walked to see the Perth Collegiate Institute. Uncle Will then asked us to mail a letter for him and gave us some money for a treat. When we came back we ran a few errands for Grandpa and at 12 o'clock had dinner. We went down to the basin at one o'clock and took us a lot of provisions which Grandma made for the "Beaver" camp.

We watched the men working at Mr. Kavanaugh's [Cavanagh][15] new yacht [and] at 2.15 started for home. On the way home the rudder broke off the "Rover" and we had a great time fixing it. It was fine and warm on the way home and we had a splendid trip. We met the "Mary Louise" on the way down. The men asked us to go again with them the next time they went up. We got home at 4.30 and went to the Ferry for provisions. When we came back we had supper and at night we made a camp fire and made porrage about 9 o'clock. Ettie, Min & Mr. McCarthy went for a row to the Ferry today.

Wednesday 10 August 1904

The down-side of their surprise visit to Perth yesterday occurred when Edmund Code's father John, being reminded of the useful help his son could provide around work and home, required his return. Edmund had to pack for home.

The large rowboat, or skiff **Jumbo**, was probably equipped with two sets of oars. Occasionally the boys are allowed to use it. Although motorboats were increasing in numbers, no cottage seemed complete without a fleet of skiffs and canoes.

The campfire recalls a long tradition of fireside reverie. Their songs and the playing of instruments was typical of generations of youngsters who had to make their own entertainment by day or evening.

After breakfast we sailed our sail-boats and helped Edmund to pack up his bed clothes, dishes etc. to take to Perth. When he was in town yesterday his father had some work for him to do as the rest of his family had returned from their visit to Innisville. Edmund brought his boat down on the Jopl yesterday to row back to-day. However he left the tent for our use and Harold, Ernie and Fred had all the bed to ourselves. After he got his goods packed we went to the Upper Locks with him to help him carry his baggage. He soon started off in his boat and we returned and played till dinner time. After dinner we

At the base of Beveridges Locks the Hicks family ventures out on skiffs, one of which is Jumbo mentioned in the diary. The steamer John Haggart, named after the man most responsible for building the Second Tay Canal (frequently called "Haggart's Ditch"), was built in Perth in 1887 and abandoned at Owen Sound in 1928, after a career of 41 years, the same number of years spent in the House of Commons by its namesake. Photo, PPC, c1899.

fixed the tent and went fishing. We had good luck and caught some fine bass. The "Mary Louise" locked through at dinner time and after it Auntie Lizzie, Ede, Bessie, Tom and Ernie went fishing in "Jumbo" while Harold and Fred fixed the tent and got supper. After supper we had a camp fire and played the mouth-organ and sang around. Ernie made a hot cup of ginger for his cold.

Thursday 11 August 1904

Provisioning a cottage or camp in the early part of the century was no easy matter. The proximity to local farmers with available produce greatly eased the burden. The Hicks cottage was not a wilderness camp relying on fish and forage, although fishing and hunting for food took place as well.

The boys were honoured that Lockmaster Buchanan had

asked for their aid, but even more so when they found that the reputation of their grandfather was so widespread. A common courtesy by Mr. McLean, living nearby at McCue, would have been a significant lesson for these youngsters that reputation and honour does reap its rewards.

The boys also visited Port Elmsley, then Pike Falls, where the First Tay Canal had its entrance locks. It was the location of saw and grist mills on the Tay River. The two-storey stone Fairgrieve and Gemmill woollen mill had been converted by 1902 into a processing mill for a local graphite mine at McCue, known as the Globe Graphite Mine, which had suspended operations between 1903 and 1908.

Since Edmund went home Tom has eaten his meals with us but he sleeps in the cottage. After breakfast we went to Mr. Buchanan's for his horse as he asked us to drive about two miles to get him some oats as he could not leave the locks on account of expecting the Westport from Perth. We hitched on to a one-horse wagon and drove to the Ferry for bread first. On the way we found a tree of choke-cherries and had a feed. We then went

Tom and Bessie Dickinson playing a game of ball in front of "Sunnybank." The ivy-like foliage acted as wind and sun-screen on the verandah. Photo, PPC, 1904.

to Mr. McLean's for the oats.[16] We were told to buy some potatoes, carrots, green tomatoes and onions for the cottage folks at some of the farms so we asked here. Mr. McLean did not have time to dig a lot of potatoes but he gave us over a peck and as we were relatives of Mr. Thos. Hicks he likewise gave us all the vegetables free. We got home at dinner time and while Fred went to get the dinner Ernie and Harold drove to Pike Fall's [Port Elmsley] to mail a letter for Mr. Buchanan. Ettie and Mr. McCarthy were fishing while we were away and caught a lot of fish. After dinner the boys had the pleasure of cleaning them. Ernie and Harold then made a charcoal stove to burn in the tent on chilly nights. We then played kick the can and after Ernie and Fred took Tom and Bessie for a row in the boat. When we came back we played foot-ball and read till supper time. After supper all the boys went for a row on the lake. While they were away we organized a band. Harold played the concertina, Ernie the drum and Fred the mouth-organ. When they returned we sang and played till bed time and then tried the charcoal stove. It burned fine but it was made out of a big paint can and the burning paint was disagreeable and nearly smothered us.

The game of "foot-ball" seems to emerge from "kick the can" on this day. Before its organization into soccer, it was often considered a ruffian's game, but it was perfect for open spaces. In a 19th century tract, W. Montague described it in **The Youth's Encyclopedia of Health with Games and Playground Amusements** as "a capital game for a large field or common, and any number on either side can play at it. Bounds being set by each of the armies, the kicking begun and the grand object will be to kick the ball over the enemy's boundary, shins occasionally suffer in the conflict, but the scuffle is very amusing."[17] Montague suggested using an Indian rubber-ball about six inches in diameter, but Fred likely used a blown animal bladder, possibly wrapped in leather.

Do we detect a note of sarcasm in Fred's voice having to

clean the McCarthy fish? And that makeshift band — just because it was home entertainment didn't necessarily mean it was good entertainment. Given that the residue in the paint cans used to provide heat was likely lead-based paint, one can imagine the impact of the toxic fumes.

Friday 12 August 1904

An interesting reference is made this day to Stonehouse Point, once part of the mainland and an island since 1872. The name refers to the warehouse and wharf built by the Tay Navigation Company soon after 1834 to be part of the Perth Landing, and the stone building used by McLaren's Distillery to ship barrels of whiskey. Because the First Tay Canal was too shallow and small to handle steamers, goods were transshipped at the point between Rideau Canal steamers and Tay Canal barges.

John A. McLaren and his Uncle, Alexander McLean, one of the local McLean clan, built a stone warehouse to transfer whiskey after the first canal became redundant. They carted whiskey over a trail to the island, a causeway that was likely flooded when the water levels rose with the raising of the Poonamalie dam in 1872. The island was also a native camping site with evidence dating back 5000 years. Indeed, Lower Rideau Lake has several important archaeological sites related to early native peoples. With the ruins of the stone house and the ancient relics, the island was a treasure trove haunted by shadows of the past.[18]

> *(Harold fell into the lake to day with all his clothes on)*
> *After breakfast the boys went back to the bush to gather pine knots. On the way back we met a big squirrel and after chasing him he ran up a tree. We threw sticks at him and tried our best to get him but he disappeared and we did not capture him.*[19] *He caused us half an hour's delay. We were back at eleven with our load and Auntie Ede, Bessie, Tom, Harold,*

Ernie and Fred rowed to the bathing-place for a swim. The water was warm and we had a fine time. While we were at the bathing place Mr. McCarthy, Ettie and Min rowed to Stonehouse Point where we find Indian relics. We were home and had our dinner over before they returned. After dinner Harold and Ernie made a better stove for the tent while Fred read in the grove. After the stove was fixed we took the large row-boat "Jumbo" and got a lot of waterlilies. We had to go through stumps and stones and we had an exciting time pushing the boat with the oars as we could not row. When we returned Harold, Ernie and Tom went for a sail on the lake.

The Hicks, Dickinson and McCarthy families enjoyed the shaded grove at "Sunnybank" cottage in summer. From left to right, Tillie, Bessie Dickinson (in hammock), Lizzie McCarthy, Will, Tom Hicks Sr. in chair, Ettie McCarthy seated in front with tennis racket, Elizabeth, Tom Dickinson seated next to Ettie, Minnie, and Harold McCarthy. Photo, PPC, 1899.

They sailed about 2 miles. Ettie, Min and Mr. McCarthy went for a walk in the groves at the Upper Locks. While we were having our supper Grandma, Uncle Will and Miss Kehoe[20] came down in the "Bessie" to take Mr. McCarthy to town as he was going to Prescott the next day. Before he went away he gave Harold, Ernie, Tom, and Fred one dollar to buy chocolates at the Ferry and gave Bessie 25 [cents]. After supper Ettie, Auntie Lizzie and Mr. McCarthy went back to Perth with them to see Mr. McCarthy off and to meet Auntie Till [Anna] from Ottawa. While they were away we washed all their dishes for them and before going to bed we made a lot of ginger.

Saturday 13 August 1904

Every summer has its cool, wet days — godsend for farmers and a day inside the tent for campers.

We wakened at 7 o'clock but it was raining so we lay in bed till nearly nine. We were kindly invited to have breakfast in the cottage as we could not cook in the rain. After breakfast we carried water for the folks and ate apples. We then played quoites and tried to ring about 12 jack-knives with small wooden rings. We had dinner at 2.30 and after dinner played and read till supper time. After supper the "Bessie" boat locked through with Uncle Will, Ettie, Mr. Bill Griffith and Auntie Lizzie.

Sunday 14 August 1904

At the turn of the century, reading and singing hymns accounted for some form of prayer or worship on a Sunday. However, although the Sabbath was strictly enforced as a day of rest by churches in the 19th century, people in general were beginning to challenge the interpretation of rest and reflection, to include the pursuit of leisure activities. The Rideau Canal locks were closed on Sundays, although some were allowed very early morning and late evening access by 1908.[21]

Tom Dickinson would later remember attending the Presbyterian Church (now Bethel United) at McCue on the

Rideau Ferry Road. Although the Hicks and Dickinson families were Anglican, any church service in proximity of the cottage was sufficient for their purpose.

(yacht raced us)
    We slept in the cottage last night as Uncle Will and Mr. Griffith occupied our tent. The latter two were up early and took the yacht for a ride away up past the Ferry. When they returned they had breakfast and after breakfast Uncle Will took Tom and Bessie for a ride in the yacht letting Tom and Bessie steer. When they came home Harold, Ernie and Fred went back to the bush and got twisted walking sticks. We were home in

Jack Griffith in the stern joins Tom Jr. and Will Hicks for some Tay Marsh duck hunting in the Bessie. Photo, PPC, c1901-1907.

time for dinner and after dinner we read till three o'clock. At three Mr. Ben Wright[22] and his mother drove out here and Mr. Wright, Ernie, Tom, Bessie, Ettie, Harold, Min, and Uncle Will went in the yacht about six miles up the lake and returned at 5 o'clock. After supper Mr. Wright and his mother went home and at seven o'clock Uncle Will and Mr. Griffith started for Portland in the yacht about 14 miles up the lake to see some man on business. After sleeping in the yacht that night they hired a horse and drove to Elgin where the man lived. After they went we sang hymns and played the mouth organ until bed-time.

Monday 15 August 1904

Ho for the Rideau! The Rideau Lakes were large enough to enjoy excursion steamers, but even more significantly, they incorporated a canal system that ensured new places to explore just beyond the next set of locks.

Today the boys finagled their way onto a civic holiday excursion to Newboro being conducted by the Freemasons, a widespread fraternity with secret customs and a high public profile.[23] The Masonic excursion was advertised for two weeks in the local papers, but it almost didn't happen. As late as Saturday afternoon, the trip suffered the rumour of cancellation owing to Captain Ned Flemming's reluctance to challenge "Haggart's Ditch" as the Second Tay Canal had come to be known.[24]

The Tay marsh had always been a shallow and dubious passage in the canal and the captain worried about a fully loaded boat scraping against real or imagined obstructions, especially in August when water levels were normally lower. Local persuasion saved the day, and ironically, Flemming did get stuck on a sand bar west of Craig Street in Perth, at 7 am, without anyone but the crew on board. This led to a delay in boarding as 250 excursionists were forced to walk from the basin south to Craig Street, where the steamer would go no further. The steamer embarked at 8:30 am, a half hour later than scheduled, and arrived at the Beveridges Locks at 9:30, without mishap.

On this excursion, the Masons and their families would be dressed in their Sunday finest — men in suits and waistcoats, and women in white flowing dresses with parasols in hand. They were on display, and they would be marched into Newboro by the local brass band.

In Newboro, main street buildings were festooned with bunting and flags. The agricultural grounds, described in the local paper as "a beautiful grove," formed the centre of a huge picnic. Races and games were held, topped off by a competitive baseball game between Perth and neighbouring Elgin costing between ten and fifteen cents for admission.

Newboro's two finer hotels looked after catering, with refreshments also served on the boat. It was a festive occasion, and spirits were high: Edwardian town and country at its best.

Fare from Perth was 75 cents, from Beveridges Locks 60 cents, from Rideau Ferry 50 cents and children were charged 25 cents fare. Advertising in the Perth **Courier** claimed 300 adult tickets and 30 children's tickets were printed "so there is no danger of the boat being overcrowded." Evidently they were not up to speed for the pranks, trickery and deception displayed by members of the "Beaver Camp."

The boys got their chance to board the festooned **Rideau King** when locking down the

Ho for the Rideau

At great expense the Masons of Perth have chartered the palace steamer KING for

Perth's Civic Holiday
MONDAY, AUGUST 15

and will run an excursion from PERTH TO NEWBORO, touching at the several points intervening, and returning by way of Portland through that picturesque spot.

AT NEWBORO THERE WILL BE

A Baseball Match

between Perth and some other team, and a good programme of other sports.

REFRESHMENTS
—Served on board.—

Fare for round trip	75c
Children under 10 years	25c
From Locks	60c
From Ferry	50c

W. J. McKerracher,
Ch. of Com.

Local newspapers in Perth ran advertisements for the Masonic excursion. This ad came from the August 12th, 1904 edition of the Perth Expositor. Photo, courtesy Hugh Henderson, Pictures Perth.

Beveridges Locks on the Tay Canal. The men and boys who got off at the upper lock were curious to see the lockage and walk a short distance on the tow path where they re-embarked below the lower lock. A good friend of the family, Mr. Jack Griffith, told the boys how they could simply mingle with the Perth crowd without being asked to show a ticket.

The voyage took them to Rideau Ferry and the swing bridge, through the northeastern extension of Big Rideau Lake and the Rocky Narrows. Then they cruised into the wide, island-studded portion of the big lake before arriving at the Narrows Lock. There they entered Upper Rideau Lake, guarded at either ends at the Narrows Lock and Newboro Lock by wooden blockhouses. (These were designed to defend the locks at the height of land and headwaters of the Rideau and Cataraqui Rivers as they descended to Ottawa and Kingston respectively.)

On Upper Rideau Lake Fred and the others saw the forested ridge of Foley Mountain which forms a backdrop to the village of Westport. Near Newboro they entered a narrow excavated channel known as the Isthmus where many canal workers died from malaria when the Rideau Canal was being built.

On the route they passed families of common loons, still a frequent site on the waterway, and saw fishermen trolling for lake trout, known locally as landlocked salmon. At the Rocky Narrows the lake depth drops to 300 feet providing an important habitat to Big Rideau lake trout and whitefish.

As to-day was civic holiday in Perth the Masons there ran an excursion on the Rideau King away up the lake about 25 miles from the locks to Newboro. The Rideau King locked through going to Perth this morning before we were up. The boat left Perth at 8 a.m. with about 300 merry excursionists and at 10 a.m. we heard it blow for the locks. Harold, Ernie, Tom and Fred hurried to the Upper Locks to meet Auntie Till and see some of the people on it. When we were near the locks we met about 50 men and boys who had got off the steamer at the Upper Locks and were walking down to the Second Locks among whom was Mr. Jack Griffith. He knows us all well as he sometimes comes down to the cottage in the yacht with Uncle Will. He called us to one side and told us a good plan how to have a free trip to Newboro. We had no intention of going and were soon in high spirits.

He said that before the excursionists got on the boat in Perth they gave their tickets to the man at the door as they always do at a show or circus and they were not given any return tickets. At Newboro any person could get on and go to Perth free whether they belonged to the crowd or not and the boat-men [stewards] would not know but what they came from Perth in the first place. He said that Harold, Ernie and Fred could get on the boat when it came to the Second Locks with all the men and boys who had walked down. So the three of us hustled to the cottage and got permission to go. In about two minutes we had our Sunday clothes on. We grabbed our purses for fear of having to pay and made a bee line for the locks just

The Rideau King was the Edwardian steamer on which Fred enjoyed his exciting excursion. Postcard by Clifford Pennock, Chaffey's Lock, c1903-1909.

as the boat got in. We mingled in with the men and boys who had walked down and when they got on we got on too. Everything went all right and no person knew but what we got on at Perth, and we saved our fare and were each 60c ahead. The three decks were crowded and a lot of people had not seats. After we started from the locks we soon reached Rideau Ferry. A lot of people had tickets bought here and were all ready to get on. The boat was so crowded that only one-half were allowed on. While we were here Fred caught sight of Mrs. Pratt and Mrs. Johnston[25] on the wharf with Mrs. Frank Pratt.[26] They saw Ernie and I also and came over to the boat to see us, and we had a good chat with them. As I had not received a letter from Papa for quite a while I was wondering if all were well and they told us that they were fine when they left Kemptville two days before. We soon left the Ferry and when Fred was walking on Second Deck some girl asked him if Fred Dickinson was his name. He told her it was but that he did not know her. She said she was Lena Furny,[27] the servant girl we had for a couple of years in Perth. As I said before Newboro is 25 miles up the lake and as we had never been up more than 10 or 12 miles we enjoyed the trip fine as the scenery on Upper Rideau Lake is magnificent. On the top deck the Perth Citizen's Band enlivened the crowd with music and on the second deck the piano and violin chimed together. Now and then we would meet a yacht and would salute it. Again we would catch sight of a family of loons swimming about near the boat and when we reached Rocky Narrows the fishermen could be seen hauling in the big salmon. The three of us climbed on the top deck where the band was an[d] enjoyed the sun and wind. We saw Miss Essie Sanders on the boat also with a lady and two children. She got on at Foster's Point where the lady she was with has a beautiful cottage.[28] After locking through the Narrows Lock we soon reached Newboro at 1:15. On the boat we bought a lot of peanuts and had a time eating them. At Newboro wharf the Brass Band of that place escorted the people up town. After going up town we walked around viewing the *principal streets and soon began to feel hungry. As we had no time to get a lunch before starting from the locks we went and had ice-cream and chocolates although this kind of a lunch was not very strengthening it suited us perfectly. Just a few minutes after having the cream the Rideau Queen blew for the Newboro Locks. We ran to the locks and got on it and sailed to Newboro wharf. It is a larger boat than the King and very pretty. We went all through it. Harold knew the "Purser" on it and he asked us if we would like to go home on it but we did not go for fear something might happen if we did. The Rideau King would be back first as the Queen had to go to Westport and Portland and the Cottage folks would wonder where we were.*

While we were at Newboro the Perth Baseball Team played the Elgin team on the Newboro Agricultural Grounds. Perth was victorious and defeated Elgin by 13 runs to one. We did not go to see the match. At a quarter after three the King blew and at 3:30 we were on our way home. We got some sandwiches on the boat and were not very hungry till we reached the locks. We arrived at the Cottage at 6 o'clock. Uncle Will and Mr. Griffith had returned from Portland just about an hour and were going to lock through to Perth soon. They took the ladies out for a little sail on the lake and met the "Aileen" Mr. Kavanaugh's new yacht heading for Perth. They returned and locked through with them. We got on the "Aileen" at the first lock and went to the Upper Locks on it. It is a fine steady boat with a 32 h.p. engine and will carry over a hundred people. On it was Johnny Conway who worked for papa and Uncle Sid[29] in Perth. He inquired after all. After they started and were out of sight we came home and had some supper and were soon in bed after an unexpected fine day's trip which cost the three of us only 50 cents instead of two dollars.

In a later issue of the Perth **Expositor**, editor Charles F. Stone (1869-1938), himself a cottager on nearby Otty Lake, described the trip as "one of the most successful excursions conducted for several years." His description amplified Fred's observations:

"The sail up the Rideau was greatly enjoyed, the many handsome and pretty cottages along the shore adding to the beauty of the the scene. Arriving at Newboro the preparations made by the good people of that pretty village completely astonished the visitors. At the wharf were a goodly number of ladies and gentlemen, boys and girls from the village, and a cordial welcome was extended to all excursionists. Nor was that all—The Newboro brass band numbering seventeen instruments was there, to enliven the day's proceedings with sweet strains of music. The members of the band wore neat costumes of blue cloth, with gold braid and hats to match, and they were untiring in their efforts to please the visitors. The welcoming crowd and the uniformed band was a big surprise, but the walk through the town elicited further exclamations of a pleasant character, and on all sides the people of Newboro were voted all right. On two of the streets arches had been erected, and in front of the Hotel Rideau and the Ontario [Hotel] were smaller arches and the word 'welcome' told the Perthites that their Newboro friends welcomed them in an open manner. The Newboro band escorted the excursionists to their hotels where dinner was served, and it must be said of the hotel proprietors, that the bill of fare was good and the services could hardly be improved upon."[30]

Tuesday 16 August 1904

After yesterday's excitement, today was an anti-climax. It was a rain day involving games to be played inside the tent and cottage.

After breakfast Ernie, Harold and Fred sailed to the Ferry for provisions. We took such a long time that we did not return till after dinner. When we got home it started to rain and owing to the kind-heartedness of the cottage folks we were not compelled to cook our own dinner. They had everything ready and all we had to do was set our table. Austin Bothwell and Christabel Bothwell[31] *from Perth and a Mr. Ross from Montreal paddled down from Perth in their canoe this morning and were having dinner when we got home. They are friends of Ettie's and played all afternoon and after supper they returned home. It rained nearly all afternoon and we played games in the tent. At about 4 o'clock it stopped raining and Harold, Ernie, Tom, and Fred went fishing. Ernie caught two large Oswego [largemouth] bass and Tom had good luck also. After supper we had a game of "pit" and Bessie, Auntie Min and I went trolling and Ernie, Harold and Tom went fishing. They caught 3 large bass and a big mud-pout.*

Elizabeth "Lizzie" Hicks McCarthy, the mother of Harold and Ettie, who originally purchased the cottage property in 1899 is seated in front of "Sunnybank." Photo, PPC, 1904.

Wednesday 17 August 1904

Before the widespread use of wooden or plastic fish lures, live bait was the only sure method of catching sports fish. We know the boys gathered worms, but Ernie had apparently set a net for minnows, a surefire way of baiting lines for action.

Auntie Till, or Annie, who worked in Ottawa for the Post Office Department had arrived for some holidays at the cottage with her mother. Instead of taking their horse Nellie with their own carriage, they hired Peter McTavish, a liveryman, who had a type of job common to rural towns and villages. They stabled the horses of visitors and kept horses for hire, not unlike a combination of today's car rental and taxi service.

Mon. Aug 15 1904

As to-day was civic holiday in Perth the masons there ran an excursion on the Rideau King away up the lake about 2 ½ miles from the locks to newboro. The Rideau King locked through going to Perth this morning before we were up. The boat left Perth at 8 a.m. with about 300 merry excursionists, and at 10 a.m we heard it blow for the locks. Harold, Ernie, Tom and Fred hurried to the upper Locks to meet auntie Jill and see some of the people on it.

Fred Dickinson's diary is a compact volume exhibiting wonderful penmanship for a boy just turning sixteen years old.

Before we were dressed the "Mary Louise" locked through going to Perth and soon we had breakfast and after going through the regular routine of washing dishes and firing out bed-clothes Ernie and Harold had the pleasure of cleaning the fish they caught last night. We then went fishing again and caught a lot of moon fish. After we came home we put up the sail and went for a sail. There was a strong breeze and we had

When were near the locks we met about 50 men and boys who had got off the steamer at the Upper Locks and were walking down to the Second Locks among whom was Mr Jack Griffith. He knows us all well as he sometimes comes down to the Cottage in the yacht with Uncle Will. He called us to one side and told us a good plan how to have a free trip to Newboro. We had no intention of going and were soon in high spirits.

He said that before the excursionists got on the

an exciting time. When we returned Ernie caught about 30 minoes [minnows] for fishing with and put them in the fish boat. After dinner Ernie, Harold and Fred sailed to Mr. Miller's for potatoes and then Ettie, Auntie Min, Bessie, Tom and the three campers went to the bathing-place for a swim. When we came back we had some fun killing a big snake. Bessie['s] rubbers were sitting on the crib-work and took a tumble in. The three of us then walked to Miller's to get bread. After supper Auntie Till and Grandma drove out with

Mr. McTavish[32], a liveryman, and Ettie returned with him. We played flinch till bedtime.

Thursday 18 August 1904

All diary writers have their lapses, and today Fred was busy catching up. It is hard to know whether they were trapping squirrels for their fur or the fun of it, but Fred has already written about terrorizing a squirrel for a half hour and beating a snake to death. The boys lost their tent temporarily and had to pile into an already crowded cottage.

Bessie Dickinson at "Sunnybank" with the entrance to the Tay Canal locks in the background. Photo, PPC, c1901.

After breakfast the Mary Louise locked through going up the lake to Portland and after it locked through the "Bessie" boat blew. In it were Mr. Tom Code[33], Mr. John Code[34], Mr. McEwen[35], and Uncle Will. They were going up the lake about 10 miles to the Rocky Narrow[s] to spend a couple of days salmon fishing. Mr. John Code owns the tent that we used and had to take it up the lake with him to sleep in. He soon had it rolled up and started on their trip. Harold, Ernie and Fred had to sleep in the tent [cottage] till they returned. After dinner we went back to the bush to trap squirrels and back there we made a large evergreen wreath for the cottage and also cut some twisted vines for snakes. When we came home we played football and ate apples, and then Fred busied himself writing his diary which he had neglected for the last few days. After supper we played New York and Fred made a lot of taffy on our stove. We had a great time pulling it and eating it. We then played tag by moon-light until after ten.

Friday 19 August 1904

Since they received a small amount of money every time they went for provisions, it was a considerable incentive to enjoy and anticipate these outings. Fred describes a keen interest in candy and chocolates, evidently passed down through the family.

We did not get up till nearly nine o'clock and after the dishes were washed we rowed to the Ferry for provisions. We stayed around the Ferry until noon and then put up the sail and sailed the whole way home. Auntie Till gave us some money for a treat and we ate the candy on the way home and also treated the Cottage folks to chocolates. When we reached home our dinner was all ready. We set our table in the grove where it was nice and shady. We had an elephant dinner bananas and pork and beans being on the list. After dinner Harold, Ernie and Fred went for [a] sail on the lake in the

The Hicks family frequently ventured out over the Rideau Lakes in their motorboat Bessie. Photo, PPC, 1904.

sail-boat. We came back in about half an hour and Ettie, Auntie Min, Bessie and we three went to the bathing place for a swim. We had a fine time and when we returned we had supper. After supper we had a game of foot-ball. Tom and Fred stood Ernie and Harold and after a very fast game Tom and Fred beat the other fellows five goals to three. While we were playing foot-ball the "Bessie" boat with the salmon fishers who went up the lake a day ago in it blew for the locks. I wrote a post-card to papa then and Uncle Will mailed it in town. They had a good day's outing and brought home some salmon also Mr. Code left the tent off for our use and after carrying it home we had to put it up again, before dark. We managed to fix it alright and then we had to get our quilts and blankets out of the Cottage and make up our bed. After we got the tent fixed we played New York and played the mouth-organ till bed time. After we went into the tent Fred complained of a sore foot. When he examined it there was a big piece of stick [a sliver] in it. Ernie went into the Cottage and got a needle and Fred worked at his foot for a long time. We intended having a game of flinch but could not it was so late. As Fred could not get the stick out he went into the cottage and the doctor (Grandma) examined it and put a poultice on it.

Saturday 20 August 1904

Late August in eastern Ontario provides a hint of fall in cool evenings, and the experience of autumn temperatures on damp days. The "Beaver" camp is not impressed with this shift in fortunes, and retreats to the glowing fires of the cottage stoves. "New York," which the children played on Friday, August 19, was likely a poker game played with regular cards. On Wednesday and Saturday, they played "Flinch," a card game with a unique set of cards, and "Fan Tan," a Chinese gambling game still remembered in the area.

"Pit" was possibly a game of marbles described as "Pits" by Alice B. Gomme in her **Traditional Games of England, Scotland**

and Ireland, where she described it being played by Cornish fishermen.[36] Cultural transfer, or traits characteristic of the immigrants' homeland that are transported to a new environment, as in the Hicks family from the borderlands of Cornwall and Devon, was part of a process which built a foundation for activities in games, songs, and lore that continued for generations.

It started to rain at one o'clock last night and was raining hard when we wakened. We lay in bed and played flinch till ten o'clock. The rain came through the air-holes in the top of the tent and as my boots were underneath them it formed a little lake in them. We then got dressed and made a buck-dart for the Cottage in the rain and we were kindly invited to visit them for the day. We had breakfast at half past ten and then we put on a good fire in the little stove in the Cottage and a good one in the kitchen. Auntie Min played "Flinch" "pit" and "Fan Tan" with us in the kitchen where it was nice and warm. A person cannot imagine unless he has been there how chilly and cold it is on the lake shore especially on a day like this. It rained all morning and at 4:30 we had dinner and after dinner Ernie and Harold sailed to Millar's for butter and eggs. After dinner

Photo "solid comfort" taken near the shore of Lower Rideau Lake shows Will Hicks relaxing with a magazine. Will was an early example of the "weekend man." Photo, PPC, c1904.

we read in the Cottage and at seven o'clock Grandma made a lot of gruel for us. We tried puzzles until bed-time.

Sunday 21 August 1904

In spite of living and camping near water, most of the Hicks family were not known for swimming skills. Indeed, in 1904, many people feared the water and could not swim. Camps and cottages increased the recreational side of swimming as a sport and method of relaxation. It was no surprise then that the boys had Auntie Min and Bessie "as white as ghosts" skimming across the waters of Lower Rideau Lake.

As Fred describes, the boys had become proficient sailors during the month.

We were up early and had breakfast and after breakfast Uncle Will and Mr. Bob Meighen came down in the yacht. Then Harold, Ernie and Fred went for a sail on the lake. We sailed to Mr. Jones' Cottage which is a very pretty one. They have a bridge made out of cedar trees and numerous cedar seats. We landed there and went back in the woods and got a lot of birch bark for note-paper. Mr. Meighen walked to the Ferry while we were away. We came home and had dinner and took then Bessie and Auntie Min for a sail while Tom went up to the yacht with Uncle Will. We then came in and got Auntie Lizzie into the boat. We sailed

Tom and Bessie Dickinson sharing a picture book on the cottage verandah. Photo, PPC, c1903.

away out on the lake where it was rough (the lake is three miles wide where we are) and we had the ladies scared. Every time we turned to tack against the wind the sail would turn and you would split laughing to see them turn pale. They turned as white as ghosts while we laughed and enjoyed the excitement. Harold, Ernie and Fred are now expert sailors and we had the laugh on them.

After we came home we all read in the grove where it is nice and cool until supper time. After supper Mr. Bob Meighen sailed from the Ferry to go up with Uncle Will to night in the yacht. About half past six Uncle Will, Auntie Lizzie, Grandma and Mr. Meighen went to Perth in the yacht. While the folks were up at the locks seeing them off we opened their provision box and procured a good supply of eating apples.

Monday 22 August 1904

Experienced boaters on the Rideau Canal are always aware of the fury that winds can produce on the inner lakes. Whitecaps foam and boats are tossed in a storm. Because Lower Rideau Lake is shaped like a deflated football (the Canadian version), winds can blow unabated across its wide middle. A sailor's delight, but a challenge in a storm!

Unlike Big Rideau Lake with its deep bays and shorelines, Lower Rideau Lake is in part, a drowned land created by the nature of the Rideau Canal as a slackwater canal, where navigation is created by raising water levels from one dam back to the next. The flooding created underwater forests of trees frozen in time. They had stood in 1832 while being flooded, eventually toppling over, and then forming a graveyard in shallow bays off the main channel. Canal engineers had little insight or concern that navigation could in the future include the entire lake. The channel was navigable, and that was all that a commercial canal required.

The Aileen the new Perth yacht owned by Mr. Kavanaugh ran an excursion from Perth this morning up the lake. She

An aerial view of Rideau Ferry and Lower Rideau Lake looking toward Poonamalie Locks on the horizon. Courtesy, National Air Photo Library, Natural Resources Canada, HA38.2., 1925.

locked through about eight o'clock. There was a very high wind blowing and the lake was as rough as we ever saw it. When the Aileen was about half way to the Ferry the row-boat which was attached to the stern of it broke loose and drifted on the lake. The water was so rough that it would have been useless to try and turn around to get it so it drifted with the waves. Auntie Ede first caught sight of it and Mr. Russell[37] the assistant lock master [lockman] came down and Ernie, Harold and Fred and he took the big row boat "Jumbo" and started for it. The waves were so high that the boat rocked like a feather on the water and sometimes the waves would come right over the side of the boat. We never had such a terrible time rowing the boat against the waves. We had to go against the waves or with them for if we had gone in the trough of them we would have been upset. The

"Aileen's" rowboat drifted away past Jones' Cottage and ran up against a lot of stumps on the shore. Soon we reached where the boat was and spent about fifteen minutes trying to get it. We rocked with the waves and pretty nearly dashed against the stumps. The rudder struck a big stone and was knocked off, and we could not fix it on again till we got home. At last Harold and Ernie caught hold of the boat and Mr. Russell and Fred rowed home. The Cottage folks were pretty afraid of the boat capsizing and watched us all the time with the big field-glass. We had to row nearly a mile and it took us half an hour to row home.

When we were nearly home it started to rain and we just reached the cottage in time to save a good drenching. When we got into the Cottage we played and sawed some wood in the kitchen. We then had a dinner in the cottage. While we were at dinner our tent blew down and the rain wet all our bed-clothes. We did not notice the tent till after the rain and then we had to put it up again. When we got it up Harold, Ernie and Fred went for a sail on the lake and on coming home Auntie Ede, Min, Harold and Fred went back to the bush for a load of pine-knots while the rest went fishing. When we came home we had supper and then the "Aileen" blew for the locks. When she went into the first lock Ernie and Harold rowed the boat in and tied it to the stem of the yacht and locked through with them. They thanked us for getting the boat as we saved them a row down in the next morning. Auntie Min, Bessie, Tom and I went up to the lock to see the passengers. Mr. Muckelson [Canon Muckleston][38] was on and we had a handshake from him. He asked how Papa was and was glad to see us all. After the "Aileen" had gone Ernie and Harold went over to Mr. Buchanan's for the mail and when they returned we played till bedtime and told stories.

One of the stories they told at night probably included the heroic effort of saving the Perth Boat from sure embarrassment. It was the kind of stirring adventure that turned excitement into tall stories.

Tuesday 23 August 1904

This was a special day for "Beaver camp." They invited the cottage folks for an evening visit to their campfire. Grandma Hicks had provided the incentive with a big bag of popcorn. The party then descended into a sugar shack feast including crackerjacks, taffy and cream candy. They also ate apples into the night.

Before we were up the Jopl and the barge Rover locked through going to Perth with a load of cheese-boxes. This is the boat that we went to Perth on two weeks ago and came back on it the same day. After we had breakfast we all went back to the

bush and spent till dinner time gathering pine-knots and wheeling them home. Harold and Fred went back for the last load and found a big birch bark tree. Fred got a piece of bark off it 4 feet long and 2 feet wide and also set a snare for a squirrel. About noon Grandma and Miss Annie James[39] drove Nellie out from Perth and stayed till after six o'clock. After dinner Bessie, Tom, Auntie Till, Miss James and Grandma went for a row to King's Point and after they came back Auntie Ede, Auntie Min, Miss James,

The top two are unidentified, but Harold McCarthy is peeking out of the "Beaver" camp tent above Edmund Code. Photo, PPC, 1904.

Bessie, Tom and we three campers went to the bathing place for a swim. After supper we went back to the bush and got more birch bark and Auntie Min, Auntie Till, Bessie and Tom went for a row. Grandma brought out a big bag of shelled pop-corn this morning and we invited the cottage folks to the camp for the evening. Ernie popped a lot of corn on our stove. It popped fine as we had the stove red hot and we had a great time eating it. Auntie Min then made a lot of syrup out of brown sugar and poured it over a lot of pop-corn. It was delicious. This mixture is what the Yankees call "Crackerjacks." Auntie Min then made a lot of taffy and cream candy and we had a swell time eating it. Auntie Till then told us a lot of stories and we had a magnificent time. We broke up the party about 9 o'clock and said good night to our visitors. Harold, Ernie and Fred then lit the lantern and after putting out the fire and tying up the tent we played flinch in the tent until ten o'clock. We then roasted some apples on the top of the lamp chimney (our lantern is a candle with a lamp chimney over it and is so arranged as to carry it by a handle) and ate them.

One wishes Fred had left a brief account of the stories Aunt Tillie told them. Were they about her great-grandfather Edward James being burned out of house and home during the violent sectarian rebellions of 1798 in Wexford, Ireland? Or Hicks memories of the downs and moors of Cornwall, and ancient Launceston Castle in the valley of the River Tamar? Were they about Fred's grandfather John Dickinson being born on a storm-tossed ship returning to Ireland from Canada in 1825 or about Grandpa Hicks arriving in Canada as a seven-year-old in 1842? Perhaps they were ghost stories about the Indian relics and stone ruins of Stonehouse Point, or the legends of ferryman John Oliver who buried his victims under his house just a little more than a mile away. Perhaps they were more recent stories about Perth, the Tay and the Rideau canals or stories about dream worlds and no place in particular.

The oral tradition of handing down stories embellished the past, carried symbols and images into the present, and helped define character and identity. Before the voice of radio or the images revealed by television, story-telling entertained and instructed. Stories came in songs, ballads, or just the tongue.

They were seldom written down, and Fred did not write the stories he heard into the journal he wrote.

Wednesday 24 August 1904

Morning chores included the woodshed and water buckets. Soft water for the washing was collected from rain-water and cisterns; hard water with iron content for kitchen use came from a local well. A provision yacht made its rounds on the lake where fresh vegetables and dairy products were sold to campers and cottagers.

Moonlight excursions were the magical tours of Ontario lakes. Centred around a couple of days preceding, during and just after a full moon, night excursions were glittering spectacles of light and dark. Shoreline campfires twinkled. If calm, the moon formed a shaft of reflecting light, if rippled with a breeze, the lake was a shimmering gleam. When lanterns were hung around the craft, it looked like a firey ghost ship from the shores. If light was extinguished, the moon cast a romantic glow over craft and passengers. The silent night was broken only by the rhythmic beat and steaming puff of the engine.

"On the verandah at Sunnybank" reveals a shaded verandah. Bessie is in the foreground, Lizzie is doing needlework, and a hammock lies invitingly behind two unidentified guests. Photo, PPC, c1904.

In 1936 Perth's W. R. Spence published his song "Moonlight on the Rideau" which evoked the charm of lakeland excursions. Moonlight excursions were the curse of lock staff expecting a

quiet night, when locks were still open for 24 hours a day
(except on Sundays).

*While Fred was cooking the breakfast Harold and Ernie
put the wood which we got yesterday into the woodshed and
after breakfast we carried water for the cottage folks to do the
washing and did little odd jobs around the cottage. Ernie and
Tom then went fishing in "Jumbo" up to the locks and just
after they had gone we heard the little yacht that goes up the
lake twice a week with corn, tomatoes, onions, peaches etc.
blowing for Mr. Ash's Cottage. So Ernie, Harold and Fred put
the sail into the boat and quickly rowed to Mr. Ash's for some
corn. It is a mile to Mr. Ash's and was good exercise for us. We
got two dozen eggs and put up the sail and sailed home. We
then ate apples and plums and worked hard at nothing until
Ernie, Bessie, and Tom went fishing in Jumbo and Harold and
Fred went for a pail of hard water. When we were going for the
water we heard the Jopl blow for the locks coming from Perth
so we went up to the Upper Locks and came down to the second
lock on it. We then had dinner and had a dandy one too. Fred
cooked a can of green peas and we had beets and canned meat
also. We ate so heartily we could hardly stand up. After dinner
Mr. McCann[40] from Perth borrowed the boat and he and his
two sons went fishing and we measured heights and polished
our boots.[41]*

Harold was 5 feet 6 1/2 inches
Fred was   5   "   3 1/2   "
Ernie "   5   "   —   "
Tom   "   4   "   4 1/2   "
Bessie "   4   "   2   "

*After this we went for a swim in the canal and had a fine
time on the raft that belong[ed] to the locks. Frank Kerr[42] and
we three turned summer-saults and dove off it and also lost the
chain off the raft. We then tried to get the chain in the bottom*

of the canal but could not so we found another chain down the pier and put it on. Mr. McCann then returned with the boat. He had fine luck and caught a lot of bass. We then took Tom and Auntie Min in the sail boat for a sail and then Frank Kerr and we three went for a sail. When we came home we had supper and Auntie Ede, Harold, Bessie, Tom, Ernie and Fred got all dressed up to go to Perth with Uncle Will should he go up at night. Uncle Will was coming down to take us to town. The boys then went up to the locks to meet Uncle Will, Auntie Lizzie and Ettie. They soon reached the locks and told us that they were not going back till morning. Not long after Uncle Will came down, the Aileen blew for the locks. It was running a moonlight excursion up the lake. We got on it at the Upper Locks and then came down to the second locks on it. They asked Uncle Will and us to go up the lake with them. Uncle Will went but we did not as it was too late and we had to be up before six the next morning. When we came home we put on a fire and had a moonlight party. Ettie made us some crackerjacks and Ernie made a lot of pop-corn. After the party we went into the tent and were soon asleep. This was our last night in the tent and we slept fine.

Thursday 25 and Friday 26 August 1904

The saddest of days at camp and cottage is the day of departure, with a flood of memories, a sense of loss, reluctant embraces, and the anticipation of home. The return for the Dickinson children was buffered by a day in Perth, exploring old and new.

They saw the newly built Lanark County House of Industry building at the edge of town. They visited the Perth Golf Links, now the oldest continuously operating course in Canada dating from 1892. Tom Code lent the children a golf club and ball. Either Tom or John Code was a runner-up club champion in 1904, scoring "42 strokes for 9 holes."[43] They also saw Perth's impressive Town Hall, constructed in 1864 and equipped with a

Downstream from the Drummond Street swing bridge in Perth, the Hicks boathouse can be seen to the right and the Beckwith Street swing bridge in the distance. Postcard, c1905.

rear bandstand where the Perth Citizen's Band played summer concerts. To this day there is still the Town Hall, a reconstructed bandstand, a continuing Citizen's Band, and open air summer concerts on Thursday evenings.

We were up before six o'clock and soon had breakfast in the cottage. Then every person came up to the Upper Locks to see us off. Before seven Auntie Ede, Auntie Lizzie, Uncle Will, Harold and Tom, Bessie, Ernie and Fred started for Perth. We arrived there at a quarter to eight and then went to Grandma's. After weighing ourselves we found that Fred gained 8 pounds, Ernie 8 lbs., Tom 3 lbs., and Harold 3 lbs. After we weighed ourselves Auntie Ede, Harold and we four went out to the Cemetry[ery]. When we were coming home Harold, Ernie and Fred walked to the "Lanark House of Industry" or "Old Peoples Home." We went all through it. There were over 30 old people spending the rest of their life there. When we got home it was nearly eleven and we ate apples and stayed around the shop until dinner time. After dinner we went down street and

bought some candy and then walked to the "Perth Golf Links."
Some men were playing and Mr. Tom Code lent us a Golf stick
and Ball and we had a great time playing around. When we
came home we had supper, and after supper we went down to
the Town Hall to see an open air concert. We came home at
9:30 and then went and had some ice-cream. The next morn-
ing we were up early and after breakfast we said good-bye to all
and thanked them for the fine visit. Grandpa gave us some
money and Auntie Ede, Auntie Lizzie and Harold came down
to the station to see us off. At 7:40 the train left and our fine
month's visit was over.

"*The End*"

The Dickinson's were swept away by rail to Kemptville where their father Benjamin, step-mother Annie, and step-brother Benjamin (Harris) waited for them. The diary was tucked away. Ettie's pictures were put in little albums. Family photographs were stored in a box — and today, mottled and faded, they provide glimpses into the summer of 1904.

Photo albums, faded pictures, and Fred's diary — all these have been re-united for this publication, a stage on which Fred sparingly, but astutely, describes his summer vacation in 1904 — an era alive with contained excitement, bursting with expectation. It was both typical of cottage life in its era and unique. It was the summer of 1904 and Fred was just having fun.

The Context
Chapter 1
Cottage Life in 1904

It is hard to determine the time when Canadians began to see the land as something more than an imposing wilderness to be cleared and tamed into rural landscapes. Canadian settlement ignored the lay of the land and carved it up as in some monstrous pie in order to control and exploit its soils, trees and minerals. In the words of Northrop Frye, it represented "the conquest of nature by an intelligence that does not love it."[44]

In the Canadian context, the sheer magnitude and necessity of creating a pastoral landscape out of the original wilderness, and the early significance of metropolitan control of the hinter-

The Grand Trunk Railway promoted Rideau Lakes tourism for its bass fishing. A guide and family stand by a rack of bass at the Opinicon Lodge at Chaffey's Lock. Postcard by Clifford Pennock, c1903-1909.

land encouraged a love-hate relationship with the land. The land was there for the taking where it could be cleared, and there to be feared where it could not, yet visitors were acutely aware of the romantic and picturesque qualities of an uncultivated panorama. Patricia Jasen has written that a unifying theme in early Ontario tourism "was the tension and interplay of notions of civilization and wildness."[45]

By the 20th century, middle and upper class Canadians in southern Ontario had found new attachment to lakeland corridors formerly raked over by lumbermen and burned over by wild fires. The accessible, controlled, and serviceable lakelands of the southern Canadian Shield emerged as "cottage country," a comfortable compromise between the search for wildness while clinging to civilization. Where the ancient bedrock of the Shield forms a mantle bordering southern Ontario, the Muskoka Lakes, Haliburton Highlands, Kawartha Lakes, and Rideau Lakes were the most significant regions developing the cottage culture of inland lakes. The lumbering frontier had moved into the new north above Lake Nipissing, leaving a near north to be manipulated in a new romance of the woods. A contradictory notion of seeking nature where the wilderness had already receded involved what Simon Schama has called "cultural reafforestation," a reviving landscape enhanced by literary and visual imagination.[46]

Being in cottage country or having northern experiences became part of what was seen as the developing Canadian character symbolized by energy, strength, health, purity, and self-reliance. The lakes, rivers and forests of the Shield provided a fertile patch of land on which to help define an authentic national legacy, the celebration of personal character, and a vigorous vision for the future.[47]

It is often been assumed that recreation in North America was invented by upper classes in the Victorian era, but the idea of vacations and leisure time was repressed by the rigours of the settlement frontier and the Industrial Revolution. According to Witold Rybczynski, "The idea of having a 'place in the country' probably entered human conciousness at the same time as people began living in cities. It was a reaction to the constraints of the rules and regulations that governed behaviour in urban society, and was also a way to temporarily escape the curbs that city living inevitably put on the individual."[48]

The purpose of having a cottage had little to do with the kinds of experiences one gets with visiting new places, but was a kind of inward journey, to discover self, nature, and unhindered relaxation. Cottage country was a place to enjoy leisure time, but it was also imbued with meaning and imagination. Young Fred Dickinson did not speculate why he was allowed to spend a vacation with family when many of his generation had neither the money or time, nor can we know whether the Dickinson or Hicks families had any ulterior motive for sending the children. We can be sure that cottage and camping experiences did have an impact on Ontario society, and that they continue to play a role in the identity of the province and the regions seasonally defined as "cottage country."

The Rideau Lakes

Much of southern Ontario was rural in nature by the 1850s. Pockets of tenacious resistence to the agrarian imperative included the Rideau Lakes region perched on the Frontenac Axis of the Canadian Shield. On many tracts of land between Cranberry and Lower Rideau Lakes, farms eked out a marginal existence until rediscovered by those seeking lakelands and lakeshores for rest and relaxation. Except for clay plains and pockets of sandy soils, the Canadian Shield was a formidable barrier to familiar settlement patterns based on farming. Lower Rideau Lake was nestled in the Smiths Falls limestone plain, a relatively flat, poorly drained region, just adjacent to the rugged shield land.

From the 1850s the Thousand Islands district of the St. Lawrence River emerged as a favourite summering ground for wealthy citizens of Canada and the United States who took advantage of the development of resorts, camps and services such as excursion steamship lines. Romantic notions of a sublime natural environment, peopled by colourful guides and boatmen and featuring a panorama of islands and rapids, provided the motivation to experience the Thousand Islands. It did not take long for the inland lakes of the Rideau Canal system to be discovered for recreational purposes.

The Garrett's Rest located on Big Rideau Lake was typical of many early resorts that catered to tourists and fishermen who gained access by way of local town steamers from Perth and Smiths Falls. Postcard, c1905.

The Muskokas experienced the first seasonal invasion of the inland lakes. As early as the 1860s tourists and cottagers were discovering the Muskoka Lakes at the outset of a "back to the land" movement. The "Muskoka Club" was founded in 1864, and in the **Guide Book and Atlas of Muskoka and Parry Sound Districts**, William Hamilton commented in 1879 "another very important and increasing multitude make Muskoka their temporary home—we mean the tourists, those birds of passage, who, like swallows, annually cool themselves by a migration to our northern vastnesses, and depart refreshed."[49]

Cottage development along the Rideau Lake shores of North Elmsley and North Burgess Townships was retarded by the great fire of 1870 which scarred the area. The Meighen family of

Perth were described as the one of the first cottagers in North Elmsley Township in 1890. A couple of decades of growth revived the character of the shoreline, making the landscape more agreeable for cottage development, and central places such as Rideau Ferry emerged as early supply and access points.[50]

The Meighen family of Perth were among the first cottagers at McLean's Bay near Rideau Ferry. This rustic shanty characterized some of the earliest Ontario cottages. Photo, courtesy of Stuart M. Douglas, c1890-1910.

The Vacation

Increased affluence, discretionary time, and more efficient access to the lakelands opened up opportunities once limited by the rhythms of work, time and space. In rural areas, summer rarely offered time for recreation, but in the towns and cities experiencing increasing industrialization, time away from bustling work-lives offered a new horizon, especially with the widespread use of Saturday afternoons for relaxation. At the turn-of-the-century, this was the beginning of the concept of the weekend. Weekend recreation was still greatly curtailed by the pious notion of religious reflection and church attendance on

Sundays, but social rigidity began offering some slack. In the words of Philippe Dube in **Charlevoix: Two Centuries at Murray Bay:** "If people still believed that an idle mind in an idle body was the devil's workshop, they were also beginning to realize the virtues of a good long rest."[51]

Recognition was given to the need for change, a healthy revival and a break from routine. In the summer of 1893 a writer commented in the Smiths Falls **Rideau Record:**

"The taking of a summer vacation has come to be a much more general practice than among the parents and grandparents of the present generation. The need of rest and recreation by those whose business cares are many, or whose sedentary habits are a tax on their strength, has almost universal recognition now, and employers show a consideration in complying with this demand, such as was not thought of in earlier and less prosperous days. They are not entirely disinterested because poor health, weak nerves, and a constant sense of responsibility, added to the wear and tear of hard work, impair the value of a man's work and mean a disastrous collapse, unless the bracing effect of well spent vacations renew the vigor of the impaired powers."[52]

The first decade of the 20th century extended the widespread notion that as the economy changed and the twin forces of urbanization and industrialization shifted families away from traditional farm labour, a new class of children, known as adolescents, were unprepared, marginalized, and vulnerable in their new setting. Especially in the case of boys, aged 12-18, who normally worked for families on the land and were perceived as gaining skills and values attained from rugged outdoor life, there was concern that town and city living led to idleness, delinquency and worse.

Youth camping was seen as a means to toughen children from non-farm settings where it was believed that, in a natural environment, they would learn useful skills when schools were closed for summer vacation. Camping and canoeing had been popular outdoor activities on Ontario lakes and rivers since the

1870s, and the creation of Algonquin Provincial Park in 1893 recognized the need to protect tracts of land for recreational purposes as well as conservation. The focus in the new decade was on the advantages for youth, and private youth camps, such as Camp Temagami which opened in 1903 in the Temagami Forest Preserve, encouraged the active enjoyment of Ontario lakelands. Although Fred Dickinson lived in the country on the outskirts of Kemptville, farming was not the primary family activity. Joining a brother, a cousin and a friend to create "Beaver" camp at the Hicks cottage was just one step, seen as a positive outlet for youth, that helped young people become attuned to the outdoors. Outdoor activities brought people closer to lakes, and encouraged a tradition of Ontario camping and cottaging that continues to define summer vacations for many families.

Vacations, travel, camping and cottaging cost money and time. For most of the population of Ontario in 1904, summer pursuits in the great outdoors was a mere dream. If not the Dickinson family in Kemptville, then certainly the Hicks family

The Bessie gave the Hicks family a ticket to ride. Like no other recreational vessel, motorboats opened the Rideau waterway. The Bessie is seen leaving Kingston Mills Locks below the Grand Trunk Railway bridge. Photo, PPC, c1904-1907.

of Perth were squarely placed in the new middle-class. Thomas Hicks Sr. had begun his own carriage factory in 1855 and built a substantial brick house in Perth in the 1870s. The factory, with several employees, was managed by his eldest son, William in 1904, and his other son, Thomas Norman, had graduated with a degree in electrical engineering at McGill University in 1902. Annie (Tillie) was a civil servant with the Post Office Department in Ottawa, and her other sisters lived at home. The Hicks family had the time, money, desire and enthusiasm to camp, cottage, and boat on the Rideau Lakes, especially when their cottage was located less than ten miles downstream from their home in Perth on the Tay River and canal.

The private cottage and motorboat revolutionized the way men and women vacationed at the beginning of the 20th century. Where public excursions, picnics, and resorts required a degree of middle-class respectability and deportment, camps, cottages, and boats allowed greater personal freedom and brought the home into the venue of the lake and forest. The cottage and motorboat excited the individualist and family-oriented notion of retreat and solitude from everyday life.

Cottages

Big Rideau and Lower Rideau Lakes were influenced by people in Perth, Smiths Falls and Ottawa venturing out into the lakes for fishing, boating and camping. Before cottages were developed as permanent stations on the shoreline, Rideau campers were comfortable with tents, especially those built on a wood platform. The summer months from the 1870s saw increased numbers camping for periods of a day to several weeks. Some camps were tent villages where extended families and friends established a home base to fish, hunt, use boats or just relax. The islands of Big Rideau Lake were mapped in 1889, and some, previously reserved for their timber rights, were made available for sale or lease from the province. There was sufficient road access around the chain of Rideau Lakes to encourage cottage clusters on the mainland, instead of sites accessible only by water. However, in rugged areas, steam engines or gasoline motors in boats were vastly more efficient than vehicles travelling by land before the First World War.

The Rideau Lakes in particular had many important advantages to people living in the corridor and planning to build a recreational retreat. G. F. McKimm, who was editor of the Smith Falls **Rideau Record** and who built a cottage on Lower Rideau Lake in the 1890s commented in 1888:

"The lake is accessible from Ottawa by rail or canal in a few hours, the surrounding country is well enough settled to furnish unlimited supplies of farm and garden produce, the waters of the lake swarm with bass and trout, and in the fall with duck, and there are broad stretches of the lake which are admirably suited for yachting.... The bold shores in many places still covered with primitive forest, clear sae-green waters and labyrinths of islands...render it a most desirable health resort for citizens who feel the necessity of stepping down from the treadmill of business once a year to hold converse with nature "and view her stores unrolled."[53]

The summer home of A. Sweet at Rideau Ferry reflects more sophisticated landscaping techniques in the lawn tennis court, but the building reflected the simplicity of early cottages. Postcard, c1905.

The "Sunnybank" cottage property was actually purchased by Elizabeth Hicks McCarthy in 1899 but was sold to her mother, Elizabeth James Hicks, in June of 1900 after the death of her husband, hardware merchant Richard McCarthy.[54] The cottage used by the Hicks' elders was the type springing up around lake shorelines to give a permanent flair to the former camps and clearings. They tended to be small, square or rectangular, structures with log, clapboard or board and batten siding, often equipped with small or spreading verandahs. Athough their purpose in part was to bring a bit of the town and city life with them, early cottagers still revelled in outdoor activities and required more permanent shelter only for sleeping, cooking and rainy days. Eventually many of these small buildings were surrounded by verandahs, which were then screened or filled-in, requiring another perimeter of open verandahs giving the building a pagoda effect as seen from the lake viewing the roofline. The Hicks cottage eventually acquired these extended verandahs, but the photos that survive from 1900 show a structure with a full length verandah across the front and a filled in section to one side.

The Hicks cottage was equipped with a cooking range and kitchen: heaven knows where everyone slept when the whole family congregated. Of the six surviving children of Thomas and Elizabeth Hicks in 1904, five were unmarried and would remain so, giving a bit of slack to accommodation demands. However, the four children of the late Ida, and two of Lizzie's and various friends, needed room; thus the existence of the tent. It would appear that a judicious time-share plan was also installed to prevent over-capacity among brothers and sisters.

Illustrations in this book show the Hicks, McCarthy and Dickinson families at recreation by their cottage "Sunnybank" at Beveridges Locks. Three of the photos date between 1899 and 1900, when recreational dress codes still insisted on long dresses for women, ties and waistcoats for men, and children decked out in Sunday clothing. Even the men boating or hunting were in their finest. This may have been the result of the presence of a photographer and camera, or a Sunday outing. Given later photographs of the older generation, it was still considered the proper dress at home or away for most of their lives. Certainly Fred Dickinson's diary tells us they had Sunday clothes for special events, but by 1904, a more relaxed dress code appeared in effect for children.

The outdoor activities of fishing, trapping, boating, swimming, using jack-knives, campfire storytelling and singsongs were obvious recreational pursuits during this period but there is evidence of newer forms of indoor and outdoor recreation. Poker was becoming popular with card games such as "New York." "Flinch" was another form of a card game and "Pit" was a game of marbles surviving from Grampa Hicks' childhood. "Fan Tan" was a Chinese gambling game. Quoits and Nobbies were ancient games passed down by the generations. The photographs of the Hicks and Dickinson families at "Sunnybank" also show tennis rackets although lawn tennis, popular since the 1880s, gets no mention. Yard games like tag, kick-the-can, foot-ball (soccer) and dress-up (note the back cover) were prevalent, but indoor board-games were still limited in scope in 1904. Family tradition has crokinole and checkers as favourite games and a Victorian board game known as "The Siege" still survives in the family cottage. Cribbage and bridge were also games played by the family, but not mentioned in the diary. Certainly cards and board games were rainy day and evening pursuits with most activities taking place outdoors. Fred's diary is evidence enough of the importance of reading and writing as a fulfilling form of recreation.

Photographs show that the adjoining grove, which offered shade from the sun, was a favourite place for outdoor relaxation. It was equipped with wooden chairs, an elaborate wooden swing and hammocks. The chairs and hammocks also appear on the verandah. The verandah is also equipped with awnings or curtains, presumably to keep out the flies on calm days and provide shade from the late-day sun. This simple wooden edifice defined the cottage in the early part of the 20th century. They became more elaborate with rising family pressures for accommodation and the reflection they had on the status of families in the community. Most of the original cottages have either disappeared or have been absorbed within larger additions that still exist. The architectural tradition of cottaging on the Rideau Lakes is rich

in form and style, but the original buildings reflect the simple needs and necessities of a family at leisure by wind and water.

Permanent cottages may owe some of their heritage to a demand by women to have a minimum standard in maintaining a site with young children. According to Charles F. Stone (1869-1938), himself a cottager on Otty Lake near Perth, he remarked in an editorial of his newspaper the Perth Expositor in 1904, that women were the main beneficiaries of the family cottage as they had the time to spend their outing with the children:

"Sunnybank" was a place where family could entertain guests. Ettie's friends crowd around a hammock. Photo, PPC, c1904-1907.

"Nearly all the cottagers have left their summer houses and returned to town. The women folk have had a good rest, and no doubt feel greatly benefited by the fresh air and freedom from social functions, but the men could now stand about two weeks of solid rest after their long summer's work at store or office, the worries and cares of providing for a home situated a considerable distance from the source of supply, and wondering if all the children will show up at the regular roll call in the evening."[55]

However, the conditions of a rustic summer home in the lakelands were not necessarily comfortable to those who had to maintain the expectations of a growing family. In the era when cottages were emerging in the lakelands, women were expected to reside at home, manage the family, and provide caregiving. As an editor in the Smiths Falls **Record News** commented in 1921:

"One wonders whether women really like camp life and if all their professed enthusiasm for it is not so much camouflage. In the case of the large majority of the occupants of these cottages and tents, they have far more comfortable quarters at home.... It may be a bold assertion to make, but it is here made in all sincerity, that the number of women going camping would be very, very small were it not fashionable to do so and were it not for the fact that camping is to their husbands and sons and daughters a source of pure delight. To married women and older daughters, who live in constant dread of snakes and poison-ivy and other evils real or imaginary, of outdoor life, camping is martyrdom."[56]

It was not just women who may fear the wild. Under a heading titled "The Vacation," a writer with the Perth **Courier** reported in 1907:

"Thousands of city people are now counting the hours when they can leave for some lake or river for an outing where they can fight mosquitos and bugs for a few days, and perhaps get drowned. It is a great thing that many of our ancestors lived and died not knowing what a vacation or outing meant."[57]

We are reminded that in spite of the lake breezes and boating, the change between house and cottage was negligible for some. Along with the amenities of home came the challenge of keeping it looking like one. The Perth **Expositor** included a poem in a July edition of the paper in 1909:

At the Summer Cottage

Father's in the woodshed
Cleaning Forty fish;
Mother's in the kitchen

Washing every dish;
Sister's upstairs making
Every bed we own;
The company is on the porch
With the Gramophone.

Father does the rowing
Brother does the chores;
Mother does the baking
Sister sweeps the floors,
Everybody's working
Here at Idlenook,
Except the company and that
Sits down and reads a book.[58]

As we will see in Fred's diary, maintaining the "Beaver" camp required the boys' active participation in food preparation, cooking, wood supply, cleaning, and airing out blankets and quilts. Their clothes, however, were still washed by the women of the cottage, and the boys fetched the buckets of water required for them to do so.

In spite of the trials and tribulations, the lakeland became a magnet, or in the words of C. L. Gilman's poem "Lure of the Open" published in **Rod and Gun in Canada**, September 1915, "It gets you at the office and/ It follows you right home." In July of 1913 a commentator in the Smiths Falls **Rideau Record** wrote:

"The busy father and the anxious mother long for July and August to get to the lake, not for the fishing, not for the company, not for the increasing appetites with fewer conveniences for satifying them; but rather for a restful, shady quiet spot where they can lounge and read or enjoy companionship, free and easy, untrammeled by padded coats and starched collars and unwatched by ever curious eyes."[59]

The cottage has become a sacred pilgrimage, a place where the pace of life changes. The senses are heightened by the sounds of nature such as wind, waves and the calls of the wild, as opposed to the more familiar sounds of home. Personal leisure grew as a Canadian priority in spite of a 19th century work ethic that pushed personal productivity and religious piety. With the rise of the weekend came the search for "A time to escape, a place to escape to" in the words of Witold Rybczynski, author of **Waiting for the Weekend.**[60] Although family members in the diary seem mostly to be enjoying several days of leisure on vacation, Uncle Will Hicks in the "Bessie" boat is clearly an early example of the "weekend man" of the 20th Century.

The spirit of revival in the lakelands of Ontario was being firmly established by an emerging middle class with time on their hands and money in their pockets. The cottage has become an extension of the city into a wilder environment, relatively remote but re-assuringly connected. The cottage has kept Ontarians associated with their natural landscape, their near north, their patient place of solitude. For Fred Dickinson and his family, the cottage remained a permanent fixture in the rhythm of a Canadian summer.

David S. Johnston wrote in "Camping on the Banks of the Rideau Lakes" in a 1909 issue of the **Rod and Gun and Motor Sports in Canada** that one of the secrets to camping is the "consoling thought that in a little less than a year we would be back again."

"In the meantime we have the memories of a glorious holiday as we have ever spent and coupled with these bright reminiscences are brilliant anticipations of similar outings. Every one who thus indulges is a convert to the pastime and once a camper always a camper is a proverb that holds good to the last. The fascinations are so strong and the advantages that follow such an outing so great that it is no wonder the number of campers grow with each year."[61]

"*To cottage* counts as a verb in some circles of society in Ontario" writes Amy Willard Cross in **The Summer House: A Tradition of Leisure**. "And of course *to summer* means a person maintains a certain residence during the hot months."[62] Whether an Ontario cottage, an Adirondack camp, a Russian dacha, or Italian villa, a home away from home usually involves a communing with nature and landscape. A railway brochure describing Ontario's lakelands commented in 1928: "Deep within the hearts of most men and women slumbers an instinct as old as humanity itself. It is the desire to renew contact with Nature, to live and to play in Nature's solitudes and recesses. It is the answer in man's soul to the lure of primeval spaces."[63]

Fred Dickinson discovered the cottage in his youth, and whether camping in a tent nearby, or sharing the hearth inside, it had an impact that lasted the rest of his life. Paula Peterson has written, "There are only those early memories: one cannot get another set—one has only these."[64] As in the words of the late Robertson Davies in his novel **The Manticore**, "I suppose unless you are unlucky, anywhere you spend your summers as a child is an Arcadia forever."[65]

Cottage country in Ontario remains a landscape frequently visited by Fred's family and descendants to this day. His experience in 1904 is at the root of a cottage tradition as strong as our northern identity and sense of place. For Fred Dickinson his diary was the beginning of an experience that lasted a lifetime.

Chapter 2
Perth, The Tay Canal, and Lower Rideau Lake

The Tay Canals

The Tay Canal is a symbol of Perth's attachment to the Rideau Canal and the corridor linking Kingston and Ottawa. In 1816 when Perth became the first of three and the major depot of the Rideau Military Settlement, the disbanded soldiers, officers and their families as well as assisted immigrants from Scotland assumed the Rideau Canal would some day be built. However, owing to prior and absentee land grants at the mouth of the Tay River, Perth was located several miles distant to Lower Rideau Lake, one of a chain of lakes that formed the headwaters of the Rideau River. The expected canal was to serve as an inland corridor away from the precarious St. Lawrence River and its proximity to the United States border. When Lieutenant-Colonel John By (1780-1836) of the Royal Engineers began supervising the construction of the Rideau Canal in 1826, Perth realized it would be located near, but not actually linked, to the waterway.

Local half-pay officer, militiaman, general merchant and politician, William Morris (1786-1858) initiated the Tay Navigation Company in 1831 to build a small branch canal from Perth to the Rideau Lakes. Using funds collected from investors, Montreal commercial houses, government grants and the sale of lots on Cockburn Island in the middle of Perth (where the Town Hall stands), the company constructed five rudimentary locks between Port Elmsley and Perth. Unlike the deep financial resources of the military-endowed Rideau Canal with its Royal Engineer designers, private contractors, steamboat-sized masonry locks, and elaborate water control systems, the Tay Canal was a mere shadow in construction techniques and canal engineering. Anticipated commercial tolls were expected to finance future improvements, but the canal remained a tortuous route through shallow swamps, providing inadequate depths to any vessels except barges. A spirited trade sustained activities between Perth and the Rideau Canal for a decade after the opening of the Tay in 1834, but the wallowing cul-de-sac degenerated into a mere timber slide by mid-century.

Perth's isolation from the waterway was compensated in part by its successful role as a local market town and the advantage of being the administrative centre for the large Bathurst District in Upper Canada. As resource frontiers grew distant and the administrative boundaries shrank, Perth felt the pressure of being restrained by location. A branch of the Ottawa and Brockville Railway, opened in 1859, offered some reprise, but potential for manufacturing growth needed the Canadian Pacific Railway which was constructed between Montreal and Toronto through Perth and Smiths Falls in the early 1880s. However, Perth never forgot that enterprise on the Tay River—the old basin sat as a permanent reminder in the heart of town. The nearly defunct Tay Navigation Company continued to rake in tolls from passing timber over its dams, with little incentive to revive the canal until John Graham Haggart (1836-1913) was elected to Parliament for the riding of South Lanark in 1872. It was a position he would retain until his death forty-one years later, after a career that saw him rise to consideration for leadership in the Conservative Party after the death of Sir John A. Macdonald, Canada's first prime minister.

The Tay River played a substantial part in Haggart family fortunes in Perth. John Haggart Sr. (1785-1854), an emigrant from Breadalbane, Perthshire, Scotland, had been a stonemason and contractor on the Rideau Canal and purchased in 1832, the first mills erected on the Tay River in Perth by Dr. Alexander Thom (1775-1845). A substantial series of mill buildings were erected on Haggart's Island, the ruined foundation of one still visible across

The Tay Canal Basin was located in the heart of Perth. Never a commercial success, the canal linked the town with the Rideau Lakes recreational community. Photo from "Souvenir, The Perth's Old Boys' Reunion," 1905.

from the stately Haggart mansion on Mill Street. John Graham Haggart assumed control of the mill complex in 1854, some of which was leased out when his political career intervened.

As an indefatigable supporter of Lanark County interests, Haggart was both a practical politician and a dreamer. Owing to the exploration for iron deposits in north Lanark, and the develoopment of apatite deposits in south Lanark, Haggart felt a canal would be needed to ship mineral products and provide coal to the anticipated blast furnace which would result from the iron mines. The iron mines never played out, the apatite and mica mines were small-scale, and the blast furnace never happened, but one reason for the canal was sustained. Moss Kent Dickinson (1822-1897), a former Mayor of Ottawa, a miller, forwarder and landowner in Manotick, and a fellow MP, argued for the development of the Tay River as a water supply conduit to the Rideau Canal. Dry seasons played havoc with mills and manufacturers on the Rideau River who were dependent on water for power or processing.[66]

Although supervising Department of Railways and Canals

officials were leery about the commercial impact of a new branch canal on the Rideau system, the effect on water management had support. Thus began a decade long process to build a new Tay Canal in three stages (each stage being conveniently announced just prior to federal elections). The first stage saw two new Rideau Canal standard locks built off Beveridges Bay[67] and a channel cut to the Tay marshes, thus cutting off Port Elmsley, which had been the terminal of the First Tay Canal. A dam on the river just below the channel entrance flooded the Tay back to the town. Begun in 1882, the first leg of the canal was complete by 1887, when the second leg carried the canal as far as the old basin, which was completely revamped and widened, and swing bridges then installed at Craig, Beckwith and Drummond Streets by 1890. Not be be outdone, Haggart arranged for a final leg, never completed to his mill on his island, because Parliament got a whiff of his folly and Perth and Haggart became a scandal for a short period in the House of Commons and the national press.

Sir Richard Cartwright of Kingston asked a question concerning the canal in the House of Commons in March of 1890 to the prime minister, Sir John A. Macdonald, also from Kingston. Cartwright asked: "This, I understand, is a really useful work; it drains the County of Perth [Lanark]." Macdonald responded: "It drains the public treasury pretty well." This frank rebuttal should have warned the opposition of scandal to come. However, Malcolm Colin Cameron (1831-1898), MP (West Huron), whose father by adoption, Malcolm Sr (1808-1876) had founded the Perth **Courier** in 1834 during the year the First Tay Canal opened, attacked Haggart and his conservative party in August of 1891 based on a report that the Second Tay Canal had collected a mere $58.81 in tolls in its first year:

"The whole result is that we have two little tugs, one little pleasure boat, two little rowboats, and one old scow navigating the Tay Canal. What a screaming farce...an expenditure of half a million resulting in a revenue of $58.81.... That canal, Mr. Speaker, will stand there for all time to come as it is now, a living monument of departmental imbecility if not of something worse."[68]

As the quote shows, the publicly built Tay Canal was no more a commercial success than the privately-built Tay Navigation Company canal. But like the first canal, it created activity. This time it was recreational activity as the new canal gave Perth access to the Rideau Lakes, then experiencing a wave of boaters, campers, fishermen, and excursionists seeking lake breezes and summer refreshment.

A sense of the role of the Tay River, Basin and Canal in Perth was expressed in James Kellock Robertson's **Tayville**. Robertson was born in Perth in 1885 and a contemporary of Fred Dickinson, who wrote turn-of-the-century reminiscences of his youthful experiences:

"It should perhaps be explained that Tayville [author's metaphor for Perth] derives its name from the river which, gently falling from a beautiful lake some ten miles away, on reaching the town turns into a canal and, after six sluggish miles, gives entrance through a pair of locks to the Rideau. Above the town the river, with its wooded banks and old log bridges, is a perfect paradise for canoeists. In the centre of the town the canal widens into a basin where docking and turning could conveniently be made by steam launches, excursion boats and occasional freighters which visited Tayville in the nineties. Past this basin our homeward way led us and it was a poor evening that failed to provide something of interest at this spot. If we missed the arrival home of the **John Haggart** with its excursion crowd from Jones Falls, it was always worth stopping to watch Tim McCarthy and Mike Byrne practising in their racing canoe."[69]

It was at these Beveridges Locks, the lower lock by Beveridges Bay, that the Hicks family first cottaged at "Sunnybank" on the Rideau in 1899. Their cottage site was adjacent to canal property on the same side as the lockmaster's house, where it stood until the late 1970s, when it was demolished.

When Fred Dickinson arrived for his summer vacation in 1904, Perth had a population of almost 4000 souls, the largest employer being the Canadian Pacific Railway car works which would burn later in the year. The town was already recognized for its heritage character, and tourism had begun to have an impact in servicing the seasonal use of the Rideau Lakes. The Tay Canal continued to suffer commercial apathy and in June of 1902, the Lanark **Era** commented that traffic had woefully degnerated, "instead of the stately steamer or even the awkward business-like tug the only freight moving (cheese boxes and lumber) is handled by a scow propelled by a large sail when the wind is favourable and by long poles when the wind is not in service." It is interesting to note a comment in the August 10th 1904 issue of the Perth **Expositor**, when Fred was visiting, that "quite a fleet of yachts and barges were on the Basin here on Tuesday. It looked like old times on the Tay."[70]

Rideau Ferry

The old ferry landing at a natural bottle-neck of the Rideau Lakes at Oliver's, later Rideau Ferry, preceded both the Rideau and First Tay canals. A laborious flat-bottomed ferry rowed with oars used to cross the gap before a bridge was built. It was an important link for Perth by land to Brockville and the St. Lawrence River. John Oliver, an assisted immigrant from Scotland, squatted on the site in 1818 but became "so useful to the settlement" as a ferryman that he received a license in 1820. John was murdered in 1821, and was succeded by his son William, who was murdered in 1842. Under the floorboards of the Oliver house it is alleged human bones were found, giving rise to the myth that some ferry passengers met violent ends.[71]

Archibald Campbell established warehouses at the ferry, and after 1832, they serviced Rideau Canal transshipment to and from Perth when merchants and forwarders found the First Tay Canal too unreliable. In 1874 the Department of Railways and Canals erected a long wooden bridge with a swing span for passing boats. A 501 foot iron bridge, also with a swing span, replaced the wooden structure in 1894.[72]

The Second Tay Canal helped re-invigorate Perth's attachment to the Rideau Lakes. Oliver's Ferry became a hive of recreational activity later in the century. In the 1880s, Helen Coutts (1828-1908), a daughter of innkeeper Archibald Campbell (d.1832), traded a brick dwelling for a frame structure with her sister Ann Smith.[73] With her husband John Coutts (1828-1904), Helen opened a boarding house catering to visitors from Perth, Smiths Falls and tourists attracted to the Rideau Waterway. In August of 1892 the Smiths Falls **Rideau Record** reported:

"Rideau Lake is thronged with visitors just now, and from the Ferry to the Upper Lakes the shores and islands are dotted all the way with tents and cottages. At the Ferry, the Hotel de Coutts is full to the roof and then not nearly all who apply can be accommodated."[74]

A three-storey addition to the rear of the house in 1893 added a dining room and thirty suites. The Coutt's House Hotel (or Hotel de Coutts when under the direction of Peter Coutts (1860-1928) between 1898 and 1905) became an anchor to the budding tourist industry. A dance pavilion proved a great attraction.

During the month that Fred Dickinson stayed at the Hicks cottage nearby, the Perth **Courier** noted in its social column, 12 August 1904:

"The Hotel de Coutts at the Ferry retains an old time favour with summer people and the house has been full for the season. Mr. Coutts is the most accommodating of hosts and life passes pleasantly for all at his well-known resort. The cottagers there are chiefly Perth people and all have very pretty places."[75]

The Ferry was also the site of the Perth civic holiday regatta held since 1897 that attracted thousands to see swimming and boating races. The Coutt's House Hotel, demolished in 1947, was rebuilt as the Rideau Ferry Inn which continued its dance tradition until it burned in 1984. Since 1967 Rideau Ferry has had an elevated concrete bridge, and a hotel and store continue

Oliver's, later Rideau Ferry, was a link between Perth and Brockville. By 1904, the ferry had become a seasonal community on the Rideau Lakes, centred around the Coutts Hotel. Postcard, c1900-1910.

to operate in close proximity to nearby cottages and marinas. Perth, the Tay Canal and Rideau Ferry continue to form a recreational triangle in the summer. In 1904, Fred was at one apex of the triangle at the cottage by the Beveridges Locks, connected by canal to Perth and along the north shore of Lower Rideau Lake to Rideau Ferry.[76]

Lower Rideau Lake

Fred Dickinson's diary reveals that in 1904 he was experiencing the shift of the Rideau Canal from a commercial to a recreational waterway; however, he was likely unaware of the magnitude of changes happening during the early years of a new century. He took rides on barges, excursion steamers, and private yachts, visited neighbouring farms, cottages and communities, and did all the things that made up a vacation for a boy on the Rideau in the summer of 1904.

Lower Rideau Lake, bounded by Rideau Ferry in the west and Poonamalie Lock in the east, was part of an original chain of lakes that formed the headwaters of the Rideau River. A lock at the Narrows, a bridge at Rideau Ferry, and a lock at Poonamalie created man-made boundaries for Upper, Big, and Lower Rideau Lakes. The shorelines were altered by the construction of the Rideau Canal where the Poonamalie dam raised the water levels for navigation on Big and Lower Rideau Lakes.

Around the lowlands of the Smiths Falls limestone plain, the flooding of the lower lake had a significant impact creating vast bays of drowned lands. These bays were created above Rideau Ferry as well, but with less impact where the rugged terrain of the Canadian Shield formed the shoreline. The Poonamalie dam was raised in 1872 causing even more flooding on the mainland and turning Stonehouse Point into an island. By 1904, the shoreline of Lower Rideau Lake was defined by a considerable amount of poorly drained lowland with pockets of cleared land for agriculture. Historically there had been large stands of pine and hemlock, with elm and ash swamps in the lowlands. There were no large forested areas left as in the upper lakes, but the outlet of the Tay River formed a significant wetland.

Lower Rideau Lake formed part of the southern border of North Elmsley Township which had a population of 1100 people in 1904, down from 2000 in 1851. Although almost 70 per cent of the land had been cleared by 1913, much of this was considered marginal land, and like neighbouring townships, North Elmsley experienced rural depopulation. More than half of the surviving population could trace Irish descent.

When it came to descriptive detail in the diary, Fred was a minimalist. One craves descriptions of landscape and setting, the sounds of the lake and canal, and wildlife experiences other than dead fish and terrorized squirrels. In its place, the following passages are included which were written by a contemporary fisherman from Smiths Falls, perhaps a little older, and certainly more aware of the environment around him on this section of the lakes. F. W. Lee, described a fishing trip with his father on the Tay River and Lower Rideau Lake in "Fishing on the Tay: An Ideal Day and Excellent Sport" in the August 1905 issue of the **Rod and Gun in Canada**.[77]

"Making a short cut through the lily pads and weeds we gained the channel of the river, father rowing smartly and I steering. The water was as still and black as ink and very warm. From the shore the deep bass of frogs and the mysterious cries of unseen waterfowl came to us. The tall cat tails shivered in the morning breeze. Clumps of water elm grew out of the reed banked shores to our right, the dark woods to our left threw that portion of the river into deep shadow; ahead the river twisted in and out intricately.

The red winged blackbirds sang in the elm trees, the cat bird called in the thicket, a long legged crane flapped around looking for fresh feeding spots, his legs sticking out when on the wing like two laths. The deep green of the shore was restful to the eye and all nature's noises soothed. Little waves lapped against our boat and the noise almost lulled me into a doze. I grew so lazy I did not even attempt to douse the green dragon flies as they flew to rest on my line."

On Lower Rideau Lake at the east end:

"We were now entering the drowned lands, immense areas where the water had overflowed when forced back by the dams. On both sides of the channel unsightly stumps and occasionally a weather swept tree protruded. Here wild rice and lilies flourished and a grand feeding ground for fish and fowl was created. Careful navigation, especially on dark nights, was required and many tragedies happening in the neighbourhood could be recalled.

The sun came out fiercely, making a scorching glare on the water and the clouds cleared off. The wind freshened into a gale and we experienced some uncomfortably big waves crossing the foot of the lake. Further up we could see white caps tossing against the shore. Running into a sheltered bay we made for Sand Island, where we cleaned our fish as bass do not keep well in the hot weather. We had thirteen in all, a string of which we were proud. What we did not eat ourselves we intended to give to friends.

There is much that is similar, and much that is different. The blackbirds, herons, cattails and frogs are still prevalent, the drowned lands are still difficult to navigate off channel, and the bass are still lurking in the shallows, but the leisurely pace of fishing from a rowing skiff is now drowned by a more impatient and frenetic pace of fishing from powerboats equipped with depth finders and fish trackers. There are fewer places to hide, float listlessly, and sustain solitude measured by hours."

Chapter 3
The Rideau Fleet:
Vessels using the Tay Canal
in 1904

Boats have always defined the Rideau Canal which was completed in 1832 for the passage of vessels along an inland waterway. Originally conceived as a military corridor, but giving birth to the first steamboat canal in North America, the Rideau quickly assumed the role of a commercial thruway to the interior Great Lakes before the completion of a series of canals on the more southerly and direct St. Lawrence River. Never rising to the dominance of either the Erie or Welland canals, the Rideau did sustain a local commercial role into the 20th century, before a pattern of recreational boating revived a purpose and role for the waterway.

In cottage country a motorboat was more likely to precede an automobile as the first internal combustion engine owned by a family. A team of horses is used to launch a motorboat at the isthmus in Newboro. Photo, c1905.

The Rideau Canal has seen a wide range of commercial and recreational vessels in its lifetime limited only by the operational length, width and depth of its locks and channels [locks are 112' (34.14 m) long and 28' (8.5 m) wide and have a draft of 5' (1.5m)]. In 1904, Fred was witnessing the decline of commercial vessels, the height of popularity of passenger and excursion steamers, and the emergence of the revolutionary motorboat with an internal combustion gasoline engine. This was a pattern experienced throughout the inland waterways and lakes of Ontario, except in the Great Lakes where commercial vessels doubled in size and length to feed the growth of regional industrialization and the American and Canadian wests.

Connected to Lake Ontario, The Rideau Canal did experience a plethora of boats indigenous to the waterways of North-Eastern North America including canoes, punts, skiffs, sailboats, runabouts, cruisers, yachts, and houseboats. In spite of this invasion that the canal made possible, most of the boats mentioned by Fred in his diary were built and designed on the shores of, or in proximity to, the Rideau Canal in Kingston, Newboro, Westport, Portland, Perth, and Ottawa. These vessels were indigenous to the waterway, shared design features prevalent in contemporary boatbuilding and presented characteristics unique to the region.

The "Bessie" Boat

In Fred Dickinson's diary there is mention made of the **Bessie**, the first documented gasoline-powered motorboat on the Rideau Lakes. On an April morning in 1901, Thomas Hicks Sr., and his sons Thomas and William, watched with anticipation as Newfoundland-born boatbuilder and machinist Isaac Troke launched the wooden vessel in the Tay Basin. The **Bessie** made its first sweep around the basin making a noise that would become familiar around the world. The fascination with the technology of an internal combustion gasoline engine that combined greater safety, portability, speed, efficiency and simplicity

In 1901 the Hicks family launched Bessie, the first known internal combustion gasoline-powered boat on the Rideau Lakes. Thomas Hicks Sr. and Jr. enjoy a trip on the Tay Canal. Photo, PPC, c1901-1904.

revolutionized recreational boating. The former steam and naptha yachts required large hulking engines, fat steaming boilers, a hull large enough to contain the system and patience to handle getting up the steam and suffering in proximity to heat and exhaust. While early motorboats had their own challenges, including reliability and sensitive fuels, they were an immediate hit, and boatbuilders quickly adapted changes in design to accommodate the new source and freedom of power.

John Maitland of Smiths Falls and William Laishley of Chaffey's Lock also experimented with the marine engine in 1901, an invention attributed to France's Gottlieb Daimler in 1887.[78]

The Perth **Expositor** described the almost completed Hicks boat in April, 1901:

"Mr. Thomas Hicks has his pretty little yacht almost completed, and it is admired by all who have seen it. It is 25 feet in length with 5 foot beam and built for safety and steadiness. The ribs are of choice blue oak free from joins, this making the construction very strong. The sheeting is of British Columbia cedar, seven eighths of an inch in thickness, while the trimmings are of oak. The hull is painted red and white with a narrow blue band running around the gunwhale. The bow and stern coverings are finished in oak, varnished, and a railing, with a wire netting, will extend around both, giving the yacht a finished appearance as well as acting as a guard to keep anything that might be placed on the decks from rolling off. The motive power will be a 3 horse-power gasoline engine, which is the modern power for small launches. The engine only takes up about 12 x 18 inches, and there is neither heat nor smoke from it, which makes it a most desirable power. It is estimated that the yacht will run about 8 miles an hour. The model is a handsome one and the builder, Mr. Isaac Troke, is being congratulated on all sides. He has stamped himself as a first class boatbuilder, which occupation he followed before coming to Perth. Mr. Hicks will use the yacht to go down to and from his cottage at the Rideau, and also for pleasure on the Rideau waters."[79]

Two motorboats at Beveridges Locks reflected the increasing interest in leisure boating on Ontario waterways. M. O. Hammond photo, Archives of Ontario, (AO134), 1905.

The cottage, of course, was "Sunnybank," and the family was excited to display the boat at the annual Rideau Ferry regatta, which had begun at the fledgling recreational community in 1897. Rideau Ferry was a short distance to the south from Beveridges Bay where it formed one of the necks in the chain of Rideau Lakes. A regatta highlight in the evening was an illuminated parade with a flotilla of steam yachts and other colourful craft decked out in lanterns and bunting. The **Bessie** was the new fangled boat at the regatta that night.

By 1905, the popular outdoor magazine **Rod and Gun in Canada** reported "gasoline launches are now all the rage." A total of 41 motorboats were stationed at Perth alone in 1908. The Hicks built their own boathouse between the Drummond and Beckwith Street bridges. For several years motorboating was sufficiently novel to inspire the description of outings in the social section of the local papers. In September of 1902, the Perth **Courier** commented "a party enjoyed cruising in Mr. Hicks' fine launch" where John and Thomas A. Code, N. McLenaghan, James Allan and William Hicks spent four days camping and fishing on the lakes. Motorboating opened the Rideau Waterway to people like no other craft had in the past. The private pleasure of recreational boating exploded with the access it created. The new dynamism was significant in the survival and transition of the Rideau Canal from a commercial to a recreational waterway.[80]

The "**Bessie** boat" as Fred desribes it, is featured frequently in the summer experience at "Sunnybank." It became the personal visa to the lakes enjoyed by his Uncle Will on weekends. Later changes in engines and hull design gave way to inboard and outboard engines and planing hulls on runabouts and cruisers.

Where local Rideau Canal boatbuilders had specialized in rowing skiffs (such as the **Jumbo** at the Hicks cottage) and some steamers (such as the **Aileen** and **John Haggart**), the motorboat challenged their resources. Hugh Harold opened a boatbuilding shop at Rideau Ferry in 1904 but the manufacture of engines and new designs in hulls encouraged larger manufacturing outlets. Some wooden boat-builders such as the Dowsetts at Portland, the Nichols at Smiths Falls, and Knapps in Kingston turned out motorboats but the revolution in fibreglass building materials after World War Two shifted boatbuilding into mass-production facilities. The **Bessie** was a local design adapting new technology for conditions on the Rideau Lakes. In 1901, it was an unique prototype on the system; by 1904, it had become part of the standard in recreational motorboating.

"On the Rideau" shows Lizzie McCarthy boating with her brother Tom Hicks Jr. Photo, PPC, c1907-1910.

Excursion Vessels and Town Boats

Passenger vessels travelled the Rideau Canal from its opening in 1832, but it wasn't until later in the 19th century that vessels were scheduled for purely recreational purposes. The difference was between people who had to travel, and those who wanted to. Certainly there were always travellers seeking new horizons, but the late Victorian period and especially the Edwardian era between 1901 and 1916, saw tourists discover and local residents rediscover the Rideau Waterway as a place to enjoy the beautiful scenery and lake breezes.

With only Ottawa, Kemptville, Merrickville, Smiths Falls, Perth, Westport and Kingston on railways in 1904, travel on the waterway remained largely dependent on available steamers.

Many of these steamers had dual purposes transporting people and freight. They could be divided into two classes of passenger carriers, town boats and Rideau boats. The former were based at communities such as Smiths Falls and Perth where they serviced local package freight on the lakes and scheduled passenger services with the odd advertised excursion. They tended to be small stubby double-decked steamers capable of navigating shallow areas, or steam yachts converted for general use. The Rideau boats, which could also be chartered for specific excursions, ran scheduled routes between Ottawa and Kingston, had overnight accommodation, handled general freight along the system and were large double-decked boats, limited only by the width, length and depth of Rideau Canal locks.

The Perth Boat: Aileen

The new Perth vessel described by Fred was the **Aileen**, a steam yacht built in Perth and owned by Nova Scotia born engi-

Smaller than his later vessel Aileen, Peter Cavanagh's first steamer Swan was a popular excursion vessel which ran from Perth to the Rideau Lakes from 1899 to 1901. Photo taken at Beveridges Locks, c1899-1901.

neer, Peter Cavanagh, who operated consecutively, several town boats from Perth between 1899 and 1916 including the **Katie, Swan, Arrah Wanna**, and **St. Louis**. Cavanagh and his partners serviced the Rideau Lakes in competition with Smiths Falls boats, most of which were owned by G. A. Davis, including the **Iola, Lee, Antelope, Buena Vista**, and **Victoria**, carrying package freight, cottage supplies, cottagers, campers and fishermen, and scheduling chartered excursions.[81]

On the 5th of August, 1904, the Perth **Courier** reported the circumstances of the new yacht, whose keel had been laid in May, under the headline: To Be Launched on Saturday."

"The handsome new yacht Mr. Peter Cavanagh has been building in the curling rink since the 9th of May will be ready to be launched on Saturday. The yacht is now out of the building and is being moved to the river bank. Mr, Cavanaugh says he is too busy with the moving of the craft to think about christening ceremonies, but doubtless these will be observed on Saturday. The boat is 59 feet long, 12 feet beam and 3 feet draught. A 35 h.p. boiler and 35 h.p. engine will supply motive power. The engine is a compound one and was built by Shelby Yelland of Kingston. Mr. Cavanagh expects to be ready to do yachting business in a week's time. The boat will carry about 100 people."[82]

On the 12th of August the competing Perth newspaper, the **Expositor**, gave even more detailed information:

"[Those who have seen] Mr. P. Cavanagh's trim though staunch steam yacht, the Aileen, are loud in their praises of the craft as to design, speed or safety and for general comfort.... She is sixty feet long with twelve foot beam and is built of the best blue oak. The ribs or frame work is of the same material and are built to last while the hull is made of the same wood two inches thick.... The finishing is in oak, which will be stained, and upholstered cushions will add to the comfort of the passengers. The forward cabin is to have drop curtains to be used in case of inclement weather, and in addition to the seats on either side, this cabin will be furnished with two moveable settees to extend down the centre of the boat when occasions demand it. The aft cabin is closed in, with three windows on either side, and will prove a boon to excursionists on many occasions. Off this cabin is a washroom and lavatory, and the open space in the stern makes an admirable place for a small party. A seat extends around the entire end of the yacht, giving accommodation for 20 people. The boat can conveniently carry 75 or 100 passengers.... The engine is a 35 horsepower one, new throughout, and made by Selby & Youlden, of Kingston, one of the best marine engine builders in Ontario."[83]

The summer schedule of the **Aileen** in July of 1906 included moonlight excursions on Monday and Saturday evenings for a quarter of a dollar; "Ladies Day" to Big Rideau Lake on Tuesday; to Westport on Wednesday; Portland on Friday; and available for chartered excursions on Monday and Thursday. On Wednesday and Friday the vessel could be flagged by cottagers, and parcels and passengers delivered to any accessible dock.[84]

Steam yachts were versatile, compact public boats capable of reaching most shoreline docks. They were a perfect size for the local lakes, as the recreational pressure was not nearly so demanding as that experienced in the 1000 Islands, Kawartha, or Muskoka Lakes regions. When the Victoria II replaced the larger Smiths Falls vessel by the same name in 1922, it had gasoline power, and the sleek lines of a steam yacht. The disappearance of the town boat was directly related to the rise of motorboating, and the accessibility of cottages by automobiles.

The Rideau Canal steamer: Rideau King

The vessel boarded by Fred Dickinson and his gang on the Masonic excursion from Perth on the 15th of August was the **Rideau King**. On the Rideau Canal this steamer looked like an opulent floating palace, and it did have great character, but many of the similar contemporary excursion vessels on the St. Lawrence River and Great Lakes made the **Rideau King** look short and stubby. The Rideau Canal limited the size of excursion steamers and the tourist market limited their numbers.

The **Rideau King**, originally the **James Swift**, built in 1893, had suffered a fire in Ottawa in 1901, and was refitted and renamed. Along with its sister ship, the **Rideau Queen**, built at Kingston in 1900, the vessels were the flagships of the Rideau Lakes Navigation Company, which defined passenger and tourist travel on the Rideau system between 1899 and 1916. Based at Kingston, the company had a comfortable arrangement with among others, the New York Central Railway to take tourists from Clayton, New York, through the Rideau system to Ottawa, and occasionally, the triangle route through the Ottawa and St. Lawrence Rivers. The vessel was pulled from scheduled service to handle occasional chartered excursions.[85]

Dual-purpose steamers from Perth and Smiths Falls serviced the Rideau Lakes recreational community. An unidentified steamer is shown departing Star Island and heading into the Rocky Narrows. Postcard, c1900-1910.

The opulent steamers were decked out with saloons, staterooms, and dance hall. The Edwardian decor in the decks above were a severe contrast to the hold, usually piled high with a plethora of package freight and produce being transfered along the canal, or for transshipment at Kingston, Ottawa, or

Montreal. On excursions, the hold would be cleared of everything except the ballast.

The **Rideau King** was built by Matthew R. Davis of Kingston; it was 107 feet long and a little more than 23 feet wide to fit into the Rideau locks. A description of the vessel survived from its maiden voyage as published in the Smiths Falls **Rideau Record** in 1893. Although the boat was altered after the fire of 1901, the following probably applied throughout its experience on the lakes:

"The new boat is without doubt the finest that has ever plied the Rideau, and is in every particular a first class craft.... She is beautifully finished in every particular, and the woodwork is painted white throughout. There is a handsome canopy over the staircase. The passenger cabins are all on the saloon deck and are handsomely finished. The dining room is very neatly fitted up and has seating capacity for thirty-two. There are sixteen staterooms and four family rooms with connecting doors. The ladies' and gentleman's toilet rooms are most conveniently arranged and are supplied with hot and cold water. She is lighted throughout by electricity and is heated by steam, in fact all her appointments are complete in every detail. From the hurricane deck a splendid view can be obtained, and one could not well imagine a pleasanter holiday than to take a round trip through the magnificent scenery of the Rideau Lakes on this beautiful and commodious steamer."[86]

When the boys jumped on board the **Rideau Queen** at Newboro for a short trip through the locks to the village wharf, they witnessed an even more splendid craft. The vessel, also built in Kingston by M. R. Davis, was about the same length, width and depth of the **Rideau King** but had 85 tons more gross tonnage at 350 tons. The Merrickville **Star** lavished praise on the new steamer in June of 1900:

"Staterooms, affording sleeping accommodation for 75 passengers, are large and roomy and neatly furnished. Spring beds, snowy linen, pretty coverlets and bright carpets make them most inviting looking. There is a marble wash-basin supplied with running water in every room and each is ventilated with cold air forced from below through a three inch pipe. There will be no lying awake o'nights on the Rideau Queen because of the oppressive heat of the staterooms. In addition to the ordinary staterooms there are two or three large family rooms in which every provision is made for the comfort of family parties. The saloon is luxuriously furnished in green plush with carpet to match and is well supplied with seats, couches and easy chairs. The feature of the Rideau Queen however is the dining room. It is almost twice as large as the James Swift and is a marvel of beauty and elegance. It is finished in red oak, highly polished, and is cut off from the front of the boat by a handsome grill arch flanked with plate glass mirrors.

The furniture is all in oak, the linen, silver and glassware are all shining new, every bit of linen, every piece of glass and silver bearing the name "Rideau Queen" together with the letter "N" on a pennant surmounting the crest. It is brilliantly lighted, as indeed is every part of the boat, and looked to be a most tempting place in which to discuss the excellent menu that the Queen is said to provide.... At the front on the lower deck there is a refreshment room where all soft drinks and cigars may be had. Last but by no means least is the handsome smoking room on the hurricane deck. It is large enough to hold a dozen smokers, is upholstered in leather, has glass sides and is altogether an ideal place in which to lounge and see the beauties of the Rideau."[87]

Steamers in Ontario helped define part of the mystique of travel and adventure on inland lake and canal systems. There was much in the Perth masonic excursion of August 1904 that could be compared to the mythical "Marine Excursion of the Knights of Pythias" as celebrated by author Stephen Leacock (1869-1944) in his famous **Sunshine Sketches of a Little Town** (1912). Perth and Mariposa (Orillia on Lake Couchiching) could be one and the same:

"Excursion Day, at half-past six of a summer morning! With the boat all decked in flags and all the people in Mariposa on the wharf, and the band in peaked caps with big cornets tied to their bodies ready to play at any minute!"[88]

Leacock's humour anatomized the everyday life of a typical small Ontario town by holding up a mirror to itself:

"I suppose that all excursions when they start are much the same. Anyway, on the Mariposa Belle everybody went running up and down all over the boat with deck chairs and camp stools and baskets, and found places, splendid places to sit, and then got scared that there might be better ones and chased off again. People hunted for places out of the sun and when they got them swore that they weren't going to freeze to please anybody; and the people in the sun said that they hadn't paid fifty cents to get covered with cinders, and there were still others who hadn't paid fifty cents to get shaken to death with the propellor."[89]

Leacock describes a typical scene at docking:

"I musn't even try to describe the landing and the boat crunching against the wooden wharf and all the people running to the same side of the deck and Christie Johnson [Capt.] calling out to the crowd to keep to the starboard and nobody being able to find it. Everyone who has been on a Mariposa excursion knows all about that."[90]

The Canadian Northern Railway which passed through Chaffey's Lock, Portland and Smiths Falls en route between Toronto and Ottawa beginning in 1915 contributed to the decline of steamer travel on the Rideau system, as did the automobile, the motorboat and the impact of the First World War. The **Rideau Queen** and **King** suffered the fate of many excursion steamers and schooners in being transformed into deckless barges for commercial purposes on the St. Lawrence River in the 1920s.

The excursion steamer was certainly the most extravagant vessel experienced by Fred Dickinson in 1904, followed by the town steam yacht, and his own family's unique motorboat.

However Fred describes other vessels in the diary. The commercial vessels included the **Mary Louise**, a square-sterned, sloop-rigged sailing scow built in Portland-on-the-Rideau in 1902 by Wesley Brooker. The vessel had a two horsepower steam engine and was 77 feet long and 18 and 1/2 feet wide. It operated on the Rideau system until 1909. The Perth **Expositor** announced the launching of the steam barge **Westport** on the 16th of August, 1903. Built at Westport by general merchant I. H. Arnold, it was 90 feet long and 18 feet wide and designed to navigate the Rideau and St. Lawrence canals, as well as the Bay of Quinte. Equipped with a steam engine that could power the craft to a speed of 7 m.p.h., it could carry a wide range of freight from dry goods to bulk products such as cheese, coal, flour, lumber, whiskey, and ore from local mica, phosphate and graphite mines.[91]

Fred and his mates went up the Tay Canal on the **Jopl**, a 52 foot long steam yacht built by John Paul of Newboro in 1895, and owned by William Spicer, a Newboro manufacturer in 1904. Capable of handling 40 passengers on excursions, it also transported package freight, such as cheese boxes. Cheese factories and cheese box manufacturers proliferated along the Rideau corridor, especially from the 1880s until the 1960s. The engine that Fred and his mates sat around while trying to warm up was an upright, high-pressure, six cylinder, nine horsepower steam engine built by Kelley & Beckett of Hamilton.[92]

The **Shanly** was a wooden single-screw river tugboat built in 1890 alongside the Ottawa basin on the Rideau Canal by Peter Good Waters and Edward Lynan Perkins. It was commissioned by the Rideau Canal to be the flagship of a new floating plant designed to service canal maintenance. The 60 foot long, 15 foot wide tug was expected to cruise at a speed of 25 m.p.h. and tow supplies, lock gate, dam and bridge timber, the canal dredge, and dump scows. It also had a varnished tongue-and-groove sided sleeping cabin for the Rideau Canal superintendent when conducting inspection tours on the canal. Frank Nevins was the tug master for its entire lifespan until 1907. The boat was named after civil engineers and railroad builders Francis (1820-1882) and his brother Walter Shanly (1819-1899).[93]

From rafts to steamers, boating was an essential part of the lakeland experience in Fred's time. Recreation has expanded in many directions and in different styles, but boats remain a popular mode of leisure on the Rideau Canal presently maintained by Parks Canada, a part of the Department of Canadian Heritage, as a Heritage Canal and National Historic Site.

Chapter 4
Epilogue

The diary ends in August of 1904. Soon after Fred's departure and the break-up of camp, the Hick's family all piled into the **Bessie** for a trip to Jones Falls on August the 31st, 1904. The lockmaster's journal for that day at Narrows Lock described their passing.[94] Grandpa Hicks died a year later on the 15th of September 1905, with Canon Muckleston ministering at the funeral in Perth and John Code, father of Edmund, serving as one of the pall bearers. There would be many visits to "Sunnybank" in the future for Fred, but the summer of 1904 stands out because of the diary that survives.

The legacy of boating, camping and cottaging on the Rideau Lakes was continued by the Hicks and Dickinson families after 1904. In 1918 Thomas Norman Hicks purchased a point of land in North Burgess Township near Winton's farm and the entrance to Adam's Lake which he named Pethern Point. He created the name by mixing Perth, his hometown, with the name of his father's home village in England, Petherwin Gate. He hired Milford Rabb and cousin Wesley James to erect a two-storey log chateau on the point using Adirondack cottage styles, Finnish building techniques and western red cedar from British Columbia.

The Hicks family packed up and left "Sunnybank" on Beveridges Bay to take up their new residence on the 15th of August, 1919. Fred Dickinson had taken leave from military duties to join them. The old cottage was sold to Harold Elliott Orr (it was demolished in the 1970s). Pethern Point eventually became a winterized retirement home for six members of the family, including Tom, Will, Annie, Edith and Minnie Hicks, and Harold McCarthy until the mid-1940s. The cottage has been handed down through the family, where the Dickinson,

Turner, Roelofson, Canning, and Hathaway families continue to keep an ongoing cottage diary, as a collective memory of summering on the Rideau.

Fred Dickinson's life after 1904

Fred was married in Toronto at St. Paul's Anglican Church on the 15th of June, 1918, by his uncle, the Reverend Alfred Sidney Dickinson (1869-1931) and by Archdeacon Henry John Cody (1868-1951).[95] His bride, Gladys Rowena Harcourt (1889-1974), was the daughter of Robert Brockhouse Harcourt (1862-1920) and Eleanor Copp (1861-1936).[96] Robert's father George Harcourt founded George Harcourt and Son, tailors on King Street in Toronto, still known as Harcourts Limited, "Robemakers and Tailors since 1842."

Fred started a career in financial management as a clerk with the Bank of Ottawa in Carleton Place, where he was paid four

The Dickinson family in Perth, 1897. Fred stands next to his mother Ida, and behind Bessie, while Tom and Ernest stand next to Benjamin. Photo, PPC, 1898.

dollars a week and was expected to sleep in the bank building with a gun under the pillow. After he was transferred to a bank in Ottawa, he served in the 43rd Duke of Cornwall Regiment, joining the 109th Regiment when his budding career as an accountant took him to Toronto in 1914-15. He enlisted with the 164th Halton and Dufferin Overseas Battalion in the Canadian Expeditionary Force in January of 1916 as a paymaster with the rank of Captain. A portion of Fred's war diary survives for April of 1917 which describes his voyage with the Battalion on board the troop ship **S. S. Carpathian**. As mentioned in his cottage diary, Fred was already a mouth-organist and chorister and on two occasions he gave public performances on the ship. One evening he sang in the dining saloon for the benefit of the Sailor's Orphanage. On another occasion he sang for the men assembled on the decks when entering the danger zone. Everyone had to be ready to abandon ship. He wrote on the 18th of April 1917:

"This afternoon the benefit concert was repeated for the men on the after deck. It was a great sight to see 2000 soldiers all scattered on the different parts of the deck listening to the different numbers. It made one really feel like singing."

The diary reflected from his youth, his love of music, his taste for seamanship and his fascination for boats. Just like his visit to the engineer on the Tay Canal barge, Fred investigated all parts of the ship including the engine room. He felt completely at ease on board, and stood out on deck during storms when most of the men were too ill to move.

Fred was posted to the 5th Division in England and was about to embark for France when he was called back to Canada. In order that he get some experience in the field, he was sent to France for ten days in March of 1918 where he took a tour of inspection. He joined the Field Cashier's Office in the Corps Headquaters at Camblain L'Abbe and visited Brigade Headquarters at the front. Fred saw little combat, but he did hear the bombing, and he had a wonderful experience in flying over the English Channel.

His return to Canada involved a promotion to the rank of Major, where he was expected to provide practical experience in setting up the Separation Allowance section in the Pay Directorate of the Paymaster General's Branch. The office needed specially qualified officers during demobilization to manage a staff of 900 clerks. This gave Fred the time to get married in 1918 and return to "Sunnybank" and attend the opening of the new Hicks cottage at Pethern Point on Big Rideau Lake in August of 1919. After his release in 1920, Fred continued to serve as a Major in a Toronto Officer Reserve Unit until 1936.

Fred became the manager at the prominent Toronto-Dominion bank branch at the corner of St. Charles and Yonge streets and took a seat on the Toronto Stock Exchange as a broker. The stock market crash of 1929 ruined his brokerage and greatly affected his health. The Great Depression, his losses, and losses experienced by others weighed heavily and led to bouts of depression. Fred rebounded when he joined the Harcourt's family firm where he was managing director when it became a limited company in 1934-5. Located at 103-105 King Street, now the site of the Toronto-Dominion Centre at King and Bay streets, Harcourts became famous for their design and manufacture of clerical robes.

Fred and Gladys had three children: Marjorie Eleanor Bleasdell, Dorothy Anne Desautels, and Nancy Edith McMillan, who were born in 1919, 1923 and 1930 respectively. Although they returned occasionally to the Rideau Lakes, Fred eventually established his own family retreat "Elm-Vue" at Port Bolster on Lake Simcoe.

Fred's wartime skills were required again in the Second World War when he was called up in 1942 to serve administrative posts in the No. 2 District Depot Headquaters in Toronto. During two world wars he was near the front for only ten days, but he was among the many essential officers and staff who worked behind the lines to manage the massive undertaking of a nation at war.

Owing to recurring bouts with depression, Fred was eventually institutionalized at the Whitby Psychiatric Hospital. He turned the Harcourts company over to his brother Ernest, and nephew B. Grant Dickinson, until it was sold to F. H. Dunham Ltd. in the 1950s. Fred died in Toronto on the 27th of November 1954.

Family Histories
The Hicks Family

Thomas Hicks Sr. (1835-1905) was born at Petherwin Gate on the border of Devon and Cornwall, the son of William Hicks (b. 1786) and Elizabeth Caddy. Thomas arrived in Canada with his father, a carpenter and wagonmaker, in 1842, and they had settled in Perth by 1851. Thomas set up shop as the proprietor of a carriage-making factory in 1855. The carriage manufacturing shop, which had several employees, was located on North Street between Gore and Drummond streets. Thomas Sr. married in 1860, Elizabeth James (1839-1917), born in Drummond Township, the daughter of Benjamin James (1800-1850) and Jane Kirk (1812-1881). Since 1900, Elizabeth owned "Sunnybank" cottage at the lower Beveridges Lock on the Tay Canal.

Elizabeth's grandfather Edward Sr. (1758-1835) and his wife Jane Godkin (b. 1762) emigrated from Knockadawk townland, Kiltrist Parish, near Gorey, Wexford County, Ireland, and had arrived on the second line of Drummond Township, in the Rideau Military Settlement near Perth, in 1816. It is family legend, typical of the chain migration that influenced such a large part of Irish settlement in Eastern Ontario, that the James and Dickinson families were acquainted in the vicinity of Gorey and their ancestors had fought together in Irish feuds and rebellions under the Earl of Courtown.[97]

Their children: Elizabeth (Lizzie) Jane (1860-1919), Ida Clarinda (1865-1898), Anna (Tillie) Matilda (1867-1951),

Emmeline (Ede) Edith (1870-1958), Minnie (Min) Etta (1872-1951), William (Will) Henry (1874-1939) and Thomas Norman (1876-1944).

Elizabeth (McCarthy) and Ida (Dickinson) married, the descendants of the family passing through the Dickinson name.

The Dickinson Family

Benjamin Furney Dickinson (1858-1915) was the grandson of pioneer Charles Dickinson (1782-1869) and Christianna Furney (1785-1862) who twice came out from Ireland (probably Kilowen townland, near Gorey, Wexford County) to settle in Upper Canada, first at Lamb's Pond north of Brockville in 1823, and later at Kemptville in 1831. Benjamin's father John (1825-1897) was born on the voyage back to ancestral Wexford County before the family was enticed the second time, possibly with the building of the Rideau Canal, to return to Canada. Benjamin was the eldest of seven brothers and two sisters born to John Dickinson and Eliza Tompkins (1831-1918) in Kemptville.

Benjamin Dickinson ventured to Perth from Kemptville to try his hand at operating a store when the town was undergoing a revival with the completion of the Canadian Pacific Railway in 1884 and the opening of the first leg of the Second Tay Canal in 1887. In 1886 his business was known as Gardiner and Dickinson, Perth Dry Goods Emporium. In 1894 he was described as a salesman, and a merchant again in 1898 and 1899 when operating with his brother, Alfred Sidney Dickinson (1869-1931), Dickinson Bros. general store.[98] In Perth he met Ida Clarinda Hicks (1865-1898), whom he married on the 15th of November 1887, the second eldest daughter of Thomas Hicks Sr. (1835-1905), owner of a home and carriage-factory on North Street.

Frederick Roy Dickinson was born on the second of August, 1888, followed by his brothers Ernest Hicks in 1890 and Thomas Herbert in 1894 and sister Bessie Maude in 1896, all born in Perth. However, with Ida's sudden death in 1898, the family was split with Tom and Bessie staying with the Hicks family in Perth, and Benjamin taking Fred and Ernie back to Kemptville. Benjamin and his sons eventually took over the stone house built by John Dickinson near an area on Kemptville Creek that has been known as Perkin's Mills, Kennedy's Bridge, or West Kemptville in Concession 3, lot 23, in Oxford-on-the-Rideau Township.

The family was reunited after Benjamin married a second time, to Annie Harris (1866-1914), a daughter of Robert Pearce Harris (1839-1917) and Jane Campbell (1839-1912), both born in Ireland, who ran from the 1860s, Harris & Campbell (later Harris

Dickinson family photograph in 1906 shows a confident Fred, the eldest, sitting with Bessie at his right and his step-brother Benjamin sitting to his left. Ernest and Tom stand behind. Photo, PPC, 1906.

& Barry), a cabinet-making and upholstery business with manufacturing and retail operations in Ottawa. Benjamin and Annie had one child, Benjamin "Dick" Harris (1902-1974). The Dickinsons grew up close to their maternal Hicks relatives in Perth, and so they were welcome guests at their grandparents' cottage.

The children of Ida Clarinda Hicks and Benjamin Furney Dickinson: Fred, Ernest, Tom and Bessie.

Frederick Roy Dickinson (1888-1954). See above.

Ernest Hicks Dickinson (1890-1985) married twice, Agnes Lauder (1891-1934) and Marie Baskerville (1904-1966). Ernest and Agnes had one son, Benjamin Grant. Ernest edited the Kemptville **Advance** before embarking in a career in outdoor advertising at the head of E. H. Dickinson Company Limited.

Thomas Herbert Dickinson (1894-1972) married in 1918 Dorothy Marguerite Lawrence (1896-1977) and their children are Frances Margaret Turner, Dorothy Claire Bosley, and Thomas Alan. Tom spent 58 years as an insurance underwriter with the Mutual Life Assurance Company of Canada.

Bessie Maude Dickinson (1896-1982) never married and served as a secretary in Harcourts Limited, and with the Government of Ontario office in London, England, before retiring to Perth.

The Dickinsons all found their way to Toronto from Kemptville, partly through the patronage of an old friend, G. Howard Ferguson (1870-1946) who was elected as a Conservative to the Ontario Legislature from the Grenville Riding in 1905, became a Minister of the Crown in 1914, and Ontario's 9th Premier between 1923 and 1930.[99] Fred's brother Ernest edited Howard's newspaper the Kemptville **Advance** before coming to Toronto.

The McCarthy Family

Elizabeth (Lizzie) Jane Hicks McCarthy (1860-1919) married in 1883, Richard H. McCarthy (1850-1900) originally from Ottawa, who formed a partnership with his brother-in-law

Benjamin Warren in 1882 to create Warren & McCarthy, hardware merchants, at the corner of Gore and Foster streets (now the site of James Brothers Hardware). Richard's father, John McCarthy (1817-1902), a tailor, had emigrated to Canada from Bruton, or Bruden, County Cork, Ireland. Before Richard's death, Elizabeth had purchased the "Sunnybank" property in 1899, and she sold it to her mother a year later. In 1904 she resided at the corner of North and Victoria streets while raising the two surviving of her three children.

Harold McCarthy (1888-1946) married Violet L. Coutie (1890-1942) and there were no children.

Etta (Ettie) Catherine McCarthy (1884-1937) married Fred Borbridge (1875-1939) of Ottawa and there were no children.

The Codd-Code Family

Edmund Butler Code (1890-1960), married Gwynneth Anna Mariah Baker in 1929 and they had four children: David Ernest, Jane Elizabeth, Nancy Ann, and Peter Edmund. Edmund's great-grandparents, John Codd (1797-1867) and MaryAnne Nugent (1792-1858) emigrated from Wicklow County, near the border of Wexford County, Ireland, and settled in 1816 in Drummond Township in the Rideau Military Settlement. Edmund's grandfather, William (1819-1868) married Elizabeth Hicks (1820-1895), originally from Enniskillen, County Fermanagh, Ireland, who was no relation to Fred's grandmother, Elizabeth James Hicks (1839-1917). Edmund's father was John Code (1852-1932) who married twice, Mary M. Butler (1859-1892) and Isabella M. McKinley (1871-1945). Edmund carried on a family insurance business in Perth.

Information on other individuals mentioned in the diary, when they are identified, are located within the endnotes.

Fred Dickinson as a young businessman in Ottawa. Photo, PPC, c1914.

Endnotes

1   The Edwardian era described that period of time involving the reign of King Edward VII, from the death of Queen Victoria on the 22nd of January 1901, until his death in 1910. In the Canadian context, the era may include the span of governments under Sir Wilfrid Laurier (1841-1919) from 1896 to the beginning of the First World War, and that of the progressivist era in the United States under President Theodore Roosevelt (1858-1919) between 1901 and 1909. This "Golden Age" included a greater focus and recognition of child-centred needs and activities. Children were no longer to be just seen, and not heard. This diary is one voice from that era.

2   William T. (1860-1936) and John Russell Griffith (1872-1928) were close friends of the Hicks family. Bill worked at the Hicks carriage factory and Jack was Perth's police chief from 1911 to 1927. Their ancestor Evan Griffith, born in Flintshire, North Wales, settled in the Rideau Military Settlement in 1816.

3   The church had its origins as St. Mary's, a log structure built in 1867, and replaced by the present church built in 1895 and renamed Bethel Presbyterian Church. The church became Bethel United Church after the union in 1927 and is located at the McCue intersection of county roads 1 and 18 west of the Ferry. McCue was named after William McCue (1840-1916), the local postmaster who established the Oliver's Ferry post office in 1886, which became known as the McCue post office from 1905 until its closing in 1913. Andrew Stewart, et. al, **Bethel United Church, Rideau Ferry, 100th Anniversary 1895-1995** (1995); Alan Rayburn, **Lost Names and Places of Eastern Ontario** (Toronto, Ontario Geneological Society, 1993) pp. 24, 31.

4   Anonymous, **The Boys Book of Sports and Games** (London, Ward, Lock & Co., n.d.) p. 28; See also **School-Boys' Diversions: Descriptions of Many New and Popular Sports** (London, A. K. Newman, c. 1823) p. 27; George Forrest, **The Playground: The**

Boy's Book of Games (London, G. Routledge, 1858), pp. 167-177; Charles and Mary Camden Clarke, **Many Happy Returns of the Day** (London, C. Lockwood & Co., 1859) pp. 226-227.

5   The Meighens were among the earliest cottagers on the Rideau Lakes with camps at Rideau Ferry and near the entrance to McLean's Bay, the latter dating back at least to 1890. Mary Osborne McLenaghan Meighen brought her five sons out to Canada from the Parish of Boveva, near Londonderry, Ireland, after the death of her husband, Robert, in 1838. Her eldest son Arthur (1825-1874) opened a general store in Perth in 1848, bringing his brothers William (1834-1917) and Robert (1837-1911) into the business by 1867, which then became Arthur Meighen & Bros, at the corner of Gore and Foster Streets, one of Perth's most significant merchant houses until it closed in 1930. Charles (1829-1917) was not a part of the store. Frank Stephen Meighen, "History of the Meighen and McLenaghan Families" n.d., courtesy, Alexander Reford.

6   Robert Smith (b. 1877) was superintendent of the Perth water-works and the son of Thomas Smith (b. 1848), a contractor who emigrated from Ireland in 1870.

7   King's Point is lost as a place-name in history, but it is likely on the north side of the shore of Lower Rideau Lake. Several members of the King family lived at Rideau Ferry in 1904 and James King was Lockmaster at Beveridges Locks between 1897 and 1902.

8   Mrs. Jim McCallum refers to Maggie (b. 1864) whose husband was then a foreman with the Hicks carriage works. The McCallums, both the Jim McCallum and Neil McCallum families, were close friends and employees of the Hicks in Perth. Neil, the eldest, a wagon-maker, was born in Scotland in 1857, and Jim, a blacksmith, was born in Canada in 1863 after the family had emigrated.

9   Spelled McVeety, McVeity, or McVittie, two brothers, James (b. 1802) and Simon (b. 1809), emigrated in 1820 from County Cavan, Ireland, to North Elmsley Township. James had a son (b. 1835) and a grandson (b. 1861) of the same name. A James McVeity had a farm on lot 16 in concession 7 in North Elmsley

Township through which part of the Tay Canal traversed in 1904. The farm the boys visited was either that of the grandson James who married Elizabeth Wilson, or that of his brother, Thomas Henry (b. 1868), who owned with his wife Louisa Covell, a neighbouring farm in lot 17, on which the "Sunnybank" cottage property had been originally separated in 1899. David Stager, **The James McVeety Family in Lanark County and the Simon McVeety Family in Huron County, Ontario, 1820-1980** *(Toronto, by the author, 1980)*.

10 Quotes attributed to Evell Gibbons, **Stalking the Wild Asparagus** (New York, 1962) quoted from Rebecca Rupp, **Red Oaks and Black Birches** (Pownal Vt., Storey, Comm Ltd., 1990) pg. 79. See also birchsap gingerale, **Dictionary of Canadianisms** (Toronto, W. J. Gage, 1967) p. 50.

11 Scottish-born Robert Miller (1847-1913) and his wife Sarah Dodds (1857-1935), who moved from Bathurst Township to concession 4, lot 20, of South Elmsley Township around 1895, ran a farm and sold produce on the bay which carries their name on Lower Rideau Lake. Grandson Don Miller and his family operate a market garden on the Rideau Ferry Road farm to this day.

12 Richard McCarthy lived in Prescott with his unmarried sister Jennie. The family is not to be confused with that of John McCarthy, founder of the Grenville Brewery in Prescott. Ettie and Harold's father, Richard H. McCarthy (1850-1900) died in Perth on the 13th of April 1900.

13 Lockmaster Daniel Buchanan (b. 1862) was one of six children born to North Elmsley Township farmer Daniel Buchanan Sr. (b. 1825).

14 In **Country Pastimes for Boys** (London, Longman, Green & Co., 1895), P. Anderson Graham spent a whole chapter on the making and sailing of toy-boats.

15 Peter Cavanagh (b. 1861) was a Nova Scotia born engineer who operated a town boat line with various partners in Perth from 1899 to 1916.

16 Brothers Thomas (1792-1851), William (n.d.), and Dr. John McLean (1788-1840) settled in the Rideau Military Settlement

near Rideau Ferry in 1816, 1817, and 1818 respectively. Their mother, Janet Huddleston, four brothers and two sisters, followed them to Rideau Ferry from Dunscove, Ruthwell Parish, Dumfriesshire, Scotland. McLean's Bay on Big Rideau Lake was named after the family. The Mr. McLean in the diary was possibly Dr. John's son, William John McLean (1831-1921), William's son, William Richard McLean (1827-1909) or his son Thomas A. (1881-1957), all residing at McCue. Arthur Weir McLean and Mary McLean, "A Brief Clan History: The Clan McLean," unpublished manuscript, 1983, courtesy Mary McLean.

17 W. Montague, **The Youth's Encyclopedia of Health with Games and Playground Amusements** (London, J. Williams, n.d.) pp. 9, 10.

18 See Gordon D. Watson, "Prehistoric Peoples of the Rideau Waterway," in F. C. L. Wyght, ed., **Archaeological Historical Symposium** (Rideau Ferry, 1982).

19 In some cases, hunting, trapping and chasing squirrels were activities that played a part in preparing boys for pursuing larger game in the future. It was not just a diversion, but formed a chapter in a contemporary volume of **Games and Sports for Young Boys** (London, G. Routledge & Sons, n.d.).

20 Likely Maggie (b. 1873), Matilda (b. 1879), or Florence (b. 1881), at that time of the 1901 census, the unmarried daughters of Henry and Elizabeth Kehoe, neighbours of the Hicks family on North Street in Perth in the 1901 census. Their grandfather Patrick was a wagonmaker, and their great-grandfather Henry emigrated from Ireland to Bathurst Township in 1825.

21 Owing to recreational pressure the Beveridges Locks were opened on Sundays from 1916 to 1924.

22 Benjamin Wright, descended from the family of furriers and tailors who were artisans in Perth since 1860, was visiting his mother in Perth from Great Falls, Montana, where he was a pattern-maker with a smelting works.

23 Membership in the Masons existed for men, 21 years or older, who met qualifications of character and reputation, and who believed in the existence of a Supreme Being. The True Britons' Lodge No. 14

A.F and A.M of Perth had their origins in 1818 among the disbanded officers and soldiers of the British military in the Rideau Military Settlement.

24 Edward 'Ned' Flemming (1868-1953) was the legendary captain of the **Rideau King**, later the **Rideau Queen,** and from 1921-1938, the Rideau Canal government tugboat **Loretta.**

25 Mrs. Johnston was likely related to William J. Johnston, proprietor of Reynolds and Johnston, Furniture and Undertaking of Kemptville. Fred's uncles William John (1861-1950) and Thomas George Dickinson (1867-1924) married Henrietta Reynolds (1860-1950) and Mary Ann Johnston (1866-1922) respectively.

26 Mrs. Frank Pratt was likely sister-in-law to James Pratt, a dealer in pianos, organs and sewing machines in Kemptville.

27 Lena Furny was likely an Irish relation from the Wexford County area, as Fred's great-grandfather Charles Dickinson (1782-1869) married in 1805, Christianna Furney (1785-1862) and Fred's father inherited Furney as a middle name. However, the Fournier family of Perth, was easily confused in oral pronounciation with Furney or Furny. In the 1901 Census of Canada, a Mary Furney (b. 1849) from Ireland was described as a visitor in Perth.

28 According to J. Carr Anderson's **Kemptville Past and Present** (Kemptville Telegram, 1903) the Sanders family were merchants, physicians, and dentists in Kemptville. Adam Foster (1846-1924) was seven times the mayor of Smiths Falls, a Rideau Canal captain, forwarder, coal merchant and the operator of electric power and waterworks plants in his home town. He was mayor in 1904 and built the cottage, known as "Langham Lodge" in the 1890s. Foster's point is now known as Davidsons Point, named after Smiths Falls baker Milton Davidson who purchased the property in 1919. The woman who was host at the cottage and accompanied Essie was likely Adam's second wife, Helen Keith, and their sons Irving and Kenneth.

29 John T. Conway gained experience in the Dickinson Brothers general store and went on to establish his own men's clothing store in 1907, becoming the mayor of Perth from 1919-1922. Conway's Men's Shop is a direct descendant on Gore Street. Uncle Sid is

Alfred Sidney Dickinson (1869-1931) who formed a partnership with Fred's father, Benjamin, until approximately 1900 when he was ordained as a minister in the Anglican Church. He participated in Fred's marriage ceremony in 1914.

30 Perth **Expositor**, 17 August 1904.

31 Austin M. and Christabel (b. 1884) Bothwell were the children of Thomas (b. 1853) and Christiana Bothwell of Perth. Thomas and his father Joshua (b. 1827) ran a cooperage (making casks and barrels) in Perth where the family establishment had existed since before 1851. Austin won a prestigious Rhodes scholarship to Oxford University, England, in 1906. Dana Ross was described in local papers in August of 1904 as visiting friends in Perth from McGill University in Montreal.

32 Peter Robson McTavish (1843-1920) operated a livery stable at the corner of Gore and North Streets near the Hicks home.

33 Thomas A. Code (1854-1937) initiated the woollen industry in Perth in 1876 after having moved from Innisville. By 1883 he had left a site adjoing the Haggart mills, and by the turn-of-the-century began expanding a complex on Herriott Street and another on Rogers Road. He was mayor of Perth, 1889-1890.

34 John Code (1850-1932), a brother of T. A. Code, was Lanark County Treasurer, and father to Edmund in the diary. See epilogue.

35 Unidentified. There were several McEwen/McEwan families in the area.

36 Alice B. Gomme, **The Traditional Games of England, Scotland and Ireland** (London, David Nault, 1894, republished by Thames & Hudson, 1984).

37 Later in 1904 John Russell was appointed bridgemaster in Perth, a position he occupied until 1924, passing boats through the Craig, Beckwith and Drummond Street bridges. The Perth **Expositor** claimed on June 30th 1924, that Russell retired with the "highest esteem of all the people in town" for maintaining beautiful gardens and lawns on canal lands.

38 The Reverend W. J. Muckleston (d. 1930) was rector of St. James the Apostle Anglican Church in Perth from 1893 to 1911.

39 Annie James (1875-1956) was a niece of Grandma Hicks and the

daughter of Edward (1837-1912) and Clarinda James. He ran a blacksmith shop at the corner of North and Drummond Streets in Perth. Annie married W. J. Warren in 1910 and they settled in Moose Jaw, Saskatchewan. See more information on the James family in the epilogue.

40 This is likely John McCann (b. 1841) who operated the marble works in the vicinity of North and Gore Streets in Perth, and was a neighbour to the Hicks family. He emigrated from Ireland in 1846 and had sons James (b. 1886), Edmund (b. 1884), Herbert (b. 1893) and Joseph (b. 1895).

41 Military records from the First World War acquired from the Personal Records Branch of the National Archives of Canada show Fred's adult height to be 5 feet 8 inches.

42 Unidentified. There were several Kerr families in Perth and surrounding areas.

43 A Mr. Benedict defeated a Mr. (Tom or John) Code for the 1904 club championship, Perth **Expositor**, 24 August 1904.

44 Northrop Frye, **The Bush Garden: Essays on the Canadian Imagination** (Toronto, Anansi, 1971) p. 224.

45 Patricia Jasen, **Wild Things: Nature, Culture, and Tourism in Ontario, 1790-1914** (Toronto, University of Toronto Press, 1995) p. 28.

46 Simon Schama, **Landscape and Memory** (Toronto, Random House, 1995) p. 95. For a description of the impact of lumbering and fires in one region, see C. D. Howe and J. H. White, **Trent Watershed Survey** (Ottawa, Commission of Conservation, 1913).

47 Carl Berger, **The Sense of Power: Studies in the Ideas of Canadian Imperialism, 1867-1914** (Toronto, University of Toronto Press, 1970) pp. 128-133.

48 Witold Rybczynski, **Waiting for the Weekend** (Toronto, Penguin Books, 1992) p. 171.

49 Quoted from Graham Smith, "Room With A View, Cottage Architects and Builders" in **Summertimes: In celebration of 100 years of the Muskoka Lakes Association** (Toronto, Boston Mills Press/Stoddart, 1994) p. 129.

50 See **A Brief Account of the Late Conflagration near Ottawa,**

August 17, 1870 (Misc. Pub. No. 1, Huntley Township Historical Society, 1992) pp. 13-14; Perth **Expositor**, 17 July 1919.

51 Philippe Dube, **Charlevoix: Two Centuries at Murray Bay** (Kingston & Montreal, McGill-Queen's University Press, 1990) p.77.

52 Smiths Falls **Rideau Record**, 27 July 1893.

53 Smiths Falls **Rideau Record**, 29 March 1888.

54 Records in the Lanark County Registry Office in Almonte show the original lot granted to James Beveridge in 1840. Elizabeth McCarthy purchased the property in part of half-lot 17, concession 7, North Elmsley Township, from Thomas Henry McVeety (b. 1868) and Louisa Covell McVeety (b. 1871) in 1899 for $25 (instrument #2422). It was a plot of land (125 feet by 209 feet) snuggled between the road allowance dividing concession 6 and 7 and the road bordering the Rideau Canal at Beveridges Locks. The property was sold to Elizabeth Hicks in 1900 for the same amount (instrument #2423). After the family moved to Pethern Point, the estate of Elizabeth Hicks sold "Sunnybank" in 1920 to Harold Elliott Orr (1894-1966) of Perth (instrument #3671). The property is described in those instruments, and outlined on survey maps in instrument #43332, and registered plan #27R-1854, the latter also known as "Department of Transport Real Estate Plan of Survey of Rideau Canal Reserve Lands, Beveridges Locks, T2797, surveyed by C.D. Copeland, 1971, filed at the Rideau Canal Office, Smiths Falls."

55 Perth **Expositor**, 7 September 1904.

56 Smiths Falls **Record News**, 9 August 1921.

57 Perth **Courier**, 9 August 1907.

58 Perth **Expositor**, 21 July 1909.

59 Smiths Falls **Rideau Record**, 17 July 1913.

60 Rybczynski, **Waiting for the Weekend**, p. 185.

61 David S. Johnston, "Camping on the Banks of the Rideau Lakes," **Rod and Gun and Motor Sports in Canada**, Vol. 10. No. 9, February 1909, pp. 834-836.

62 Amy Willard Cross, **The Summer House: A Tradition of Leisure** (Toronto, HarperCollins, 1992) p. 16.

63 Quoted from Liz Lundell, **Summer Camp: Great Camps of Algonquin Park**, (Erin, Boston Mills Press/Stoddart, 1994) p. 10.

64 Paula Peterson, **Coming Home: An Intimate Glance at a Family Camp in the Adirondack North Country** (Utica, North Country Books, 1993) p. 32.

65 Robertson Davies, **The Manticore** (Toronto, Macmillan, 1972) p. 72.

66 For more information on Perth and the Tay Canal, see the author's **Perth: Tradition and Style in Eastern Ontario** (Toronto, Natural History/Natural Heritage Inc., 1992); **The First Tay Canal in the Rideau Corridor, 1830-1850** (Ottawa, Parks Canada, Microfiche Report Series MF 142, 1984); **The Second Tay Canal in the Rideau Corridor, 1880-1940** (Ottawa, Parks Canada, MF 295, 1986); and biographies of Moss Kent Dickinson (Vol. XII pp. 257-259) and John Graham Haggart (forthcoming Vol. XIV) for the **Dictionary of Canadian Biography**.

67 Beveridges Bay on Lower Rideau Lake was named after James Beveridge (b. 1793) who purchased property in the bay in 1840. He was one of the assisted emigrants of the Glasgow Junior Wrights Society among the Lanark Society settlers. He came to Canada on the ship **George Canning** in 1821, settling first in Dalhousie Township. See Carol Bennett, **The Lanark Society Settlers** (Renfrew, Juniper Books, 1991) p. 112; Gerald J. Neville, **The Lanark Society Settlers: Ships' Lists of the Glasgow Emigration Society** (Ottawa, British Isles Family History Society of Greater Ottawa, 1995) pp. 20-27.

68 Canada, **House of Commons Debates**, 12 August 1891, p. 3743.

69 J. K. Robertson, **Tayville** (Toronto, Ryerson Press, 1932) p. 53.

70 Lanark **Era**, 11 June 1902; Perth **Expositor**, 10 August 1904.

71 John Oliver from Scotland took up land as an assisted emigrant in the Rideau Military Settlement in 1818. See James Kennedy, **South Elmsley in the Making 1783-1983** (Corporation of the Township of South Elmsley, 1983), pp. 17-24. The Oliver family of the ferry should not be confused with George Oliver from Jeddsborough, Scotland, who served in the Glengarry Fencibles in the War of 1812 and who settled in 1818 in Bathurst Township as

part of the Rideau Military Settlement. This latter family moved to the Rideau Ferry Road in 1828 where Don Oliver and his sons George and Bill still reside.

72 National Archives, Dept. of Railways and Canals, RG 43, Vol. 2023, part 2, pp. 331-333, Arthur T. Phillips to A. E. Dubuc, 12 Sept. 1929.

73 The Coutts family of Rideau Ferry emigrated from Coupar Angus, Perthshire, Scotland, in 1843. Peter Coutts (1798-1854) and Jeanne Geekie (d. 1848) arrived in North Elmsley Township with six children. Their son John (1828-1904) and his wife Helen, a daughter of Archibald Campbell and Elizabeth Buchanan, and grandson Peter (1860-1928) were proprietors of the Coutt's House Hotel.

74 Smiths Falls **Rideau Record**, 4 August 1892.

75 Perth **Courier**, 12 August 1904.

76 See also Mrs. Edward Joynt, "The History of Rideau Ferry," unpublished manuscript, n.d.., published in part in the Smiths Falls **Record News**, 17 February - 10 March 1966. Courtesy Murray and Kathryn Coutts.

77 F. W. Lee, "Fishing on the Tay: An Ideal Day and Excellent Sport," **Rod and Gun in Canada**, Vol. 7, No. 3, August 1905, pp.323-326.

78 Confirmation of the Hicks motorboat being the first on the Rideau Lakes is supplied by the Perth **Expositor**, 27 July 1916.

79 Perth **Expositor**, 18 April 1901.

80 **Rod and Gun in Canada**, September 1905, p. 445; Perth **Courier**, 12 Sept. 1902.

81 These vessels are discussed in Larry Turner, **Recreational Boating on the Rideau Waterway, 1890-1930** (Ottawa, Parks Canada, Microfiche Report Series MF 253, 1986) pp. 257-278.

82 Perth **Courier**, 5 August 1904.

83 Perth **Expositor**, 12 August 1904.

84 Perth **Expositor**, 4 July 1906.

85 For more information see Turner, **Recreational Boating on the Rideau Waterway, 1890-1930**, pp. 239-256.

86 Smiths Falls **Rideau Record**, 8 June 1893.

87 Merrickville **Star**, 21 June 1900.

88 Stephen Leacock, **Sunshine Sketches of a Little Town** (Toronto, McClelland and Stewart, 1960) p. 36.

89 **Ibid**. pp. 42, 43.

90 **Ibid.**, p. 46.

91 Edward Forbes Bush, **Commercial Navigation on the Rideau Canal, 1832-1961** (Ottawa, Parks Canada, History and Archaeology 54, 1981) p. 203; Perth **Expositor**, 16 August 1903.

92 Bush, **Commercial Navigation**, pp. 192-193.

93 Larry Turner, **Rideau Canal Work Vessels** (Ottawa, Parks Canada Microfiche Report Series MF 294, 1987) pp. 10-17, 160-167.

94 NA., RG. 43, Vol. 1951, Narrows Lockmasters Journal, 31 August 1904.

95 Henry John Cody was a sitting Conservative member of the legislature, soon to be Minister of Education and between 1933 and 1947, the president and later chancellor of the University of Toronto. See D. C. Masters, **Henry John Cody: An Outstanding Life** (Toronto, Dundurn, 1995).

96 Eleanor was the daughter of William W. Copp (who emigrated from Devon in 1842 about the same time as the Hicks family), a printer and bookseller who formed with Henry J. Clark in 1865, Copp Clark and Company (incorporated in 1885), a textbook firm still active in publishing.

97 For more information on chain migration, see Bruce S. Elliott, **Irish Migrants in the Canadas: A New Approach**, (Kingston and Montreal, McGill-Queen's University Press, 1988).

98 Perth **Expositor**, 22 April 1886; See also Perth assessment rolls, 1894, 1898.

99 For information on Premier Ferguson, see Peter Oliver, **G. Howard Ferguson: Ontario Tory** (Toronto, University of Toronto Press, 1977).

Larry Turner BA (Trent), B.Ed (Ottawa), MA (Queen's) is an author, educator, researcher, consultant and publisher in Canadian history. An active member of the American Association for State and Local History, the British Isles Family History Society of Greater Ottawa, the Canadian Nautical Research Society, the Champlain Society, the Federation of Ontario Naturalists, the Friends of the Rideau (past-chairman),  and the Ontario Historical Society, he was nominated with John de Visser as a finalist in the Ontario Trillium Award/Prix Trillium for **Rideau** in 1995.

This book is published without the aid of public grants or subsidy.